D0615679

The Front Part of the House and the Annex

All the above numbers also refer to specific pages of this book.

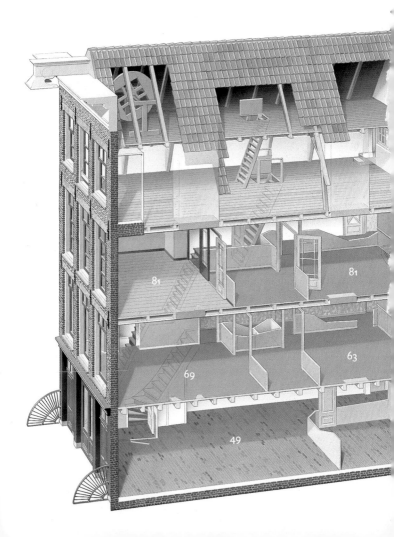

Anne Frank House
A Museum with a Story

Anne Frank

Anne Frank House
Amsterdam

House

A Museum with a Story

"One day this terrible war will be over. The time will come when we will be people again and not just Jews!" "We can never be just Dutch, or just English, or whatever, we will always be Jews as well. But then, we'll want to be."

Anne Frank, April 9, 1944

Foreword

"One day this terrible war will be over. The time will come when we will be people again and not just Jews," writes Anne Frank in her diary on April 9, 1944. At that moment around 100,000 of the 140,000 Jewish residents of the Netherlands have been deported to concentration and extermination camps. Around 25,000 Jews have gone into hiding to avoid this fate; 17,000 of them will survive the war.

The group of eight people in hiding, which included Anne, is betrayed. On September 3, 1944 they are placed on the last train leaving Westerbork transit camp headed for Auschwitz. We know that Anne died in Bergen-Belsen concentration camp in March 1945. Just a few weeks later, on April 15th, the English army liberated the camp. Of the people in hiding only Otto Frank returned after the war. He arranged the 1947 publication of Anne's diary. To date her book has been translated into approximately sixty languages.

The diary of Anne Frank ends on August 1, 1944. She left no accounting of her experiences in the German *SD*-prison in Amsterdam or of her journey through the camps Westerbork, Auschwitz, and Bergen-Belsen. Still her diary is for many of its readers a first acquaintance with this period of history. To many others, Anne Frank has become the "face" of the millions of victims of the Shoah. The writer Primo Levi, who survived Auschwitz, explained this as follows: *"One single Anne Frank*

*moves us more than the countless others who suffered just
as she did but whose faces have remained in the shadows.
Perhaps it is better that way; if we were capable of taking in all
the suffering of all those people, we would not be able to live."*

By reading Anne Frank's book or seeing the stage adaption
one is personally confronted with the reality of the persecution
of the Jews. It is therefore understandable that many people
want to see the actual hiding place where Anne wrote her
diary. Over the course of the years this interest has continued
to grow, giving rise to a paradoxical situation in which
hundreds of thousands of people per year want to visit one
of Amsterdam's most hidden and secretive places.

The Anne Frank House opened in 1960 as a small museum.
To welcome visitors, the front part of the building – the former
business premises – was rebuilt as a reception and exhibition
space. Only the back part of the house, also known as the
annex, was left in its authentic state. Between 1996 and 1999,
a new building was constructed next to the two canal-side
houses that up until that moment were the museum's home.
This facilitated returning the front part of the house to the
way it was during the hiding period. This section located in
the front of the building played an important role in the story
of the hiding period. Once the warehouse workers downstairs had gone home, the people in hiding could come out
of the Secret Annex and spend time in the work spaces and
the offices of Otto Frank's company.

Visitors to 263 Prinsengracht are taken on a journey back in time. In each of the rooms, excerpts from Anne's diary provide an impression of what happened there during the hiding period. Visitors encounter traces of the inhabitants of the Secret Annex, but also of the four employees of Otto Frank who did so much to help the people in hiding.

In compiling this catalogue, we followed the museum-route through the Anne Frank House. The quotations and objects displayed in the actual exhibition can also be found here, supplemented by background information. After the arrest on August 4, 1944, the Secret Annex was emptied of all its furnishings by order of the German Occupation authorities. To provide a better impression of the situation during the hiding period, color photographs of a temporary refurnishing of both the front part of the house and the Secret Annex, are included in this book. In 1954, black & white photographs of the Anne Frank House were made by the photographer Maria Austria. Many of these photographs also appear in this catalogue.

"We can never be just Dutch, or just English, or whatever, we will always be Jews as well. But then, we'll want to be," wrote Anne on April 9, 1944. Today people are still being persecuted and murdered because they, just like Anne, are not only "different" but also "want to be". This makes a visit to the Anne Frank House meaningful, also in our times.

Hans Westra, *Executive Director, Anne Frank House*

Table of Contents

13 A Prior History

185 After the Arrest

247 Appendix

A Prior History

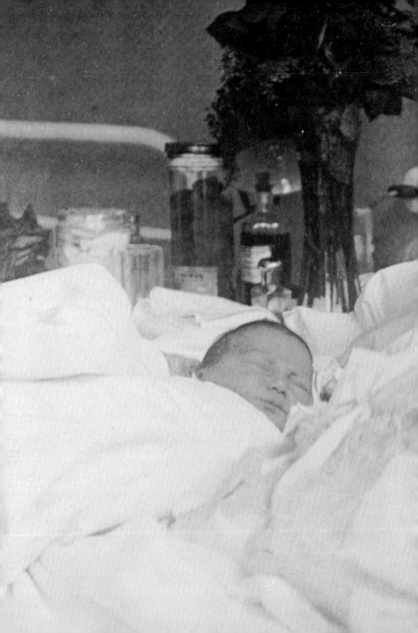

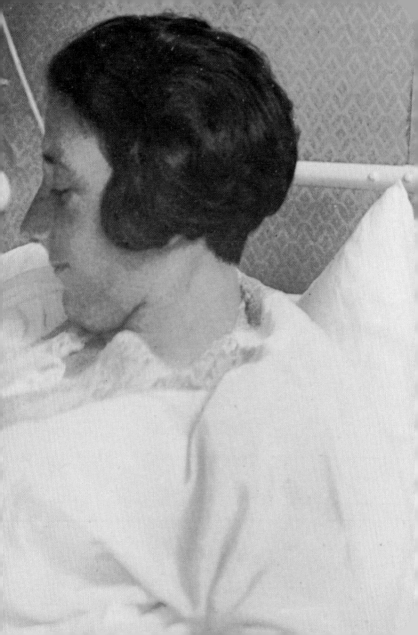

"My father, the most precious father I've ever seen, didn't marry my mother until he was thirty-six and she was twenty-five. My sister Margot was born in 1926 in Frankfurt am Main in Germany. I followed on June 12, 1929." (Anne Frank)

Otto Frank and Edith Holländer are married on May 12, 1925, Otto's birthday. The marriage takes place in the synagogue in Aachen. Nine months later, on February 16, 1926, their first daughter Margot Betti is born. Anne(lies) Marie follows on June 12, 1929. The Franks are secular Jews. Anne's parents feel connected with the Jewish faith yet are not strictly religious. Edith visits the synagogue regularly.

← Anne Frank and her mother,
  one day after Anne's birth.

1

2

1 Otto Frank and Edith Frank-
Holländer on their honeymoon
in Sanremo (Italy), 1925.

2 Alice Frank-Stern, the mother
of Otto Frank, as a hospital
volunteer, 1916.

"I wouldn't go as far as to say that I did not feel like a Jew then. Yet, in one way or another, I was consciously aware of being a German. Otherwise, I certainly wouldn't have become an officer in World War One and I wouldn't have fought for Germany." (Otto Frank)

Otto Frank identifies with being German and fights for Germany in World War One (1914-1918), just like his brothers Herbert and Robert. Otto is decorated and promoted to the rank of officer. During World War One, his mother works as a volunteer in a military hospital. Also the oldest brother of Edith, Julius Holländer, serves in the German army. He is shot in the arm during the war and is left with a stiff elbow. After the war Otto Frank, together with his younger brother Herbert, manages the family owned bank and the trade in mineral lozenges.

Germany loses World War One. The Peace Treaty of Versailles (1919) requires Germany to pay massive war reparations. The country plunges into an economic and political crisis.

3 Otto Frank as an officer, 1918.

"I can remember that as early as 1932, groups of storm troopers (Brownshirts) came marching by singing: "When Jewish blood splatters off the knife." That made it more than clear to everyone. I immediately discussed it with my wife: 'How can we leave here?', but eventually there is of course the question: How will you be able to support yourself if you go away and give up more or less everything?" (Otto Frank)

The year that Anne is born, 1929, is marked by a worldwide economic crisis. Germany is hit hard: countless numbers of businesses go bankrupt and millions of people lose their jobs. Also business at the bank owned by the Frank family is continually on the decline. By 1934 the bank will no longer exist. For Anne and Margot Frank the years in Frankfurt are peaceful, they hardly notice the crisis. Anne truly loves the stories her grandmother tells her and often plays with her sister and the children in the neighborhood. Not only Jews live in their neighborhood, but also Catholics and Protestants.

In this climate of crisis the *Nationalsozialistische Deutsche Arbeiterpartei* (*NSDAP* or Nazi party) can flourish. This small, extreme-nationalistic political party, under the leadership of Adolf Hitler, professes to have the solution to all problems. According to the Nazis, the stipulations of the Peace Treaty of Versailles should be rescinded and the Jews are the ones responsible for the lost war and for the economic and political malaise.

Otto and Edith Frank are seriously concerned about their future in Germany and that of their children.

4 Margot, Anne and Otto Frank,
1930.

5

MRZ. 10 1933

7

6

5 Anne and Edith, 1931.
6 Edith, with Anne and Margot
   on Hauptwache, a square
   in Frankfurt, March 10, 1933.

7 A snapshot of Anne, Edith and
   Margot Frank made in an auto-
   matic photo booth in the Tietz
   department store, March 10, 1933.

23

"On January 30th (1933) we were unexpectedly invited over by acquaintances. We were sitting around the table listening to the radio. Then came the news that Hitler had become Chancellor. This was followed by a report about the Brownshirt's torch lit procession in Berlin and we could hear the screaming and cheering. Hitler ended his speech with the words: 'Just give me four years.' Our host then said enthusiastically: 'Let's see what that man can do!' I was speechless, my wife stunned." (Otto Frank)

Hitler becomes Chancellor of Germany on January 30, 1933. On March 5, 1933 there are elections for the *Reichstag* (Parliament) and a week later for the local city councils. The National Socialists win both elections. Frankfurt am Main is completely decked out in swastika flags. Two days earlier, Otto takes a photograph of Edith, Anne and Margot on Hauptwache, a well-known square in Frankfurt. At that moment the decision to emigrate has probably already been made, because in March the Frank family moves in with Otto's mother to economize on their living costs.

"Because we're full-blooded Jews, my father emigrated to Holland in 1933. He became the Managing Director of the Dutch Opekta Company, which manufactures products used in making jam. In September my mother went to Holland as well, while Margot and I were sent to Aachen. Margot went to Holland in December and I followed in February, when I was plunked down on the table as a birthday present for Margot." (Anne Frank)

In the summer of 1933, Otto and Edith Frank decide to leave Germany. Thanks to his brother-in-law Erich Elias, Otto has the opportunity to set up a franchise for selling pectin. Pectin is a jelling agent used in preparing jam. Otto travels to Amsterdam first. Edith, Anne and Margot go to grandmother Holländer in Aachen. Edith commutes back and forth to Amsterdam to assist Otto in finding a suitable residence for the family. He begins building up his business. Miep Santrouschitz and Victor Kugler become trusted employees, later Jo(hannes) Kleiman and Bep Voskuijl join them. In addition, several people work for Otto's company in the warehouse and in sales.

8 Anne and Margot in Aachen,
   summer 1933.

26

10

11

9

9 Otto Frank and Miep
   Santrouschitz in the office, 1933.
10 Anne, in Mr. Gelder's
   second grade class at the
   Montessori School, 1936.
11 Peter van Pels (middle)
   and his friends in Osnabrück
   (Germany), circa 1936.

*"In the Netherlands, after those experiences in Germany, it was as if our
life was restored to us. Our children went to school and at least in the
beginning our lives proceeded normally. In those days it was possible
for us to start over and to feel free."* (Otto Frank)

The Frank family lives on Merwedeplein in a newly built neighborhood
of Amsterdam. More and more Jewish refugees fleeing Germany come
to live in the city. Anne and Margot go to school and learn Dutch very
quickly. They have both Dutch and German friends. The Frank family
keeps abreast of what is happening in Germany by corresponding
with friends there.

There are more and more measures enacted to limit contact between
Jews and non-Jews or to make it a criminal offense. These regulations are
effective even though some people do try to offer resistance. The Jews
in Germany are driven further and further into isolation.

Otto and Edith Frank meet Hermann and Auguste van Pels and their
son Peter: the future co-inhabitants in hiding. The Van Pels family has fled
Osnabrück in 1937. Hermann van Pels becomes Otto Frank's business
partner in 1938. His special knowledge of spices used for preparing
meats and sausage makes Otto Frank's company less seasonally
dependent.

→ Anne in the sandbox with
friends, July 1937. From left
to right: Hannah Goslar,
Anne Frank, Dolly Citroen,

Hannah Toby, Barbara and
Susanne Ledermann.

"Our lives were not without anxiety, since our relatives in Germany were suffering under Hitler's anti-Jewish laws. After the pogroms in 1938, my two uncles – brothers of my mother – fled and found safe refuge in North America." (Anne Frank)

During the night of November 9, 1938, 236 people in Germany are murdered and 177 synagogues, 7,500 stores, and countless number of homes are destroyed by the Nazis. Based on prepared lists approximately 30,000 Jewish men are arrested and deported to concentration camps. Among them are Anne's uncles, Julius and Walter Holländer. Julius is released right away because he is a war veteran. Walter is deported to the Sachsenhausen concentration camp. He is imprisoned for longer and is only released when he declares that he will leave Germany immediately. The magnitude of the danger is now more than apparent to them. They decide to flee Germany. Between 1933 and 1939 half of all the Jews in Germany leave the country.

Jewish refugees seem to be safe in Amsterdam. Sometimes on Saturday afternoons the Frank family holds open house with coffee and cake. There are usually numerous guests, mainly German Jews. Counted among them are: Hermann and Auguste van Pels, as well as Fritz Pfeffer and Charlotte Kaletta. Also Miep Santrouschitz and her fiancé Jan Gies are often invited.

31

12

12 Fritz Pfeffer and his Catholic
girlfriend Charlotte Kaletta.

32

13

14

15

"After May 1940 good times rapidly fled: first the war, then the capitulation, followed by the German invasion which is when the suffering of us Jews really began." (Anne Frank)

In March 1939, Grandmother Holländer flees to the Netherlands and moves in with the Frank family. She is forced to leave almost all her possessions behind. Anne and Margot are busy going to school, play a lot with their friends, and are hardly aware of the great threat. On June 12 1939, Anne Frank celebrates her tenth birthday. She invites along eight of her friends. Half of them, just like her, have recently arrived from Germany. It is to be her last birthday not clouded by wartime.

On August 23, 1939, Germany signs a nonaggression pact with the Soviet Union. On September 1, 1939, the German army invades Poland. Prominent Poles, many of them Jewish, are murdered.

In Western Europe there is little awareness of the atrocities that are being committed in Poland. Like many of the Dutch, Otto and Edith Frank assume that the Netherlands will remain neutral just like it was in World War One. Yet, in May 1940 the war begins in the West. The German Army occupies the Netherlands, Belgium, and France. However, all inhabitants are required to fill-in a so-called Aryan declaration. They have to state if they have any Jewish grandparents and if so, how many? In this manner all of the 140,000 Jews living in the Netherlands are registered.

14 The Frank family on
    Merwedeplein, circa 1940.
15 Anne Frank.

"Anti-Jewish decrees followed each other in quick succession and our freedom was strictly limited: Jews must wear a yellow star; Jews must hand in their bicycles; Jews are banned from streetcars; Jews cannot ride in cars, even their own; Jews may only do their shopping between 3:00 p.m. and 5:00 p.m.; Jews may only go to barbershops and beauty parlors owned by Jews; Jew have to stay indoors from 8:00 p.m. to 6:00 a.m.; Jews may not go to theaters, movies, or frequent any other forms of entertainment; Jews may not use swimming pools, tennis courts, hockey fields or any other sport facilities; Jews are not allowed to go rowing; Jews may not take part in any public sporting events; Jews are not allowed to sit in their gardens or those of their friends after 8:00 p.m.; Jews are not allowed to visit Christians at home; Jews must attend Jewish schools, etc. (Anne Frank)

In all of the occupied countries, one of the first steps taken by the Germans in power is the registration of the Jews. Isolation is the next step. Just like earlier in Germany, continuing steps are taken against the Jews to segregate them from the non-Jewish populace. In September 1941, Anne and Margot begin attending a special Jewish high school, the Jewish Lyceum. Throughout the city hang signs saying: "No Jews Allowed". Jews may also no longer have their own businesses. Otto Frank therefore appoints Jo Kleiman director of Opekta, but he remains active behind the scenes. Also the spice concern Pectacon changes ownership and is called Gies & Co, after Miep's husband Jan Gies. In the summer of 1941, Otto Frank begins furnishing a hiding place in the empty annex behind his company at 263 Prinsengracht.

16 Anne in her last year at the Montessori School. After the summer vacation of 1941, Jewish children must go to separate schools.

17 Miep Santrouschitz marries Jan Gies on July 16, 1942.

35

16

17

18

18 On her thirteenth birthday
Anne receives a diary as a gift.

"In the summer of 1941 Grandma (Holländer) got very sick. She had to have an operation and nothing much was done about my birthday. Also in the summer of 1940 not much of anything happened, because the war had just begun in Holland. Grandma died in January 1942. Nobody knows how often I think of her and still love her. So this birthday in 1942 was celebrated to make up for all the others, and Grandma's candle was lit along with the rest." (Anne Frank)

On June 12, 1942, Anne turns thirteen years old. On this birthday she also receives gifts from Peter van Pels and Charlotte Kaletta. Her parents give her a diary for her thirteenth birthday. In that diary she writes about everything she experiences, feels, and thinks. For a few weeks, her diary entries revolve around school, classmates and friends; after that her life changes dramatically.

By the end of 1941, the registration and segregation of the Jews in Germany and in most of the occupied territories is completed. During the secretive "Wannsee Conference" in Berlin on January 20, 1942, top Nazi officials work out the "final solution to the Jewish question". Probably the decision to murder all eleven million European Jews is taken earlier, in the summer of 1941. The plans for deportation and extermination are now put into effect. In most of the occupied countries and in Germany, Jews receive a call-up notice to report for work camps. In actuality, from the beginning of October 1941, Jews are systematically deported to concentration and extermination camps, most of which are built in occupied Poland. In these camps many people are murdered immediately or die after a short while from malnutrition, exhaustion, or diseases.

19 Anne and Margot Frank,
    circa 1942.

"Sunday morning Hello and I lay on our balcony in the sun. He was supposed to return Sunday afternoon, but instead at around 3 o'clock a police officer came to see mother and he shouted from downstairs in the doorway: 'Miss Margot Frank!'. Mother went downstairs and she got a card from the officer, written on it was that Margot Frank had to report to the SS. Mother was totally upset and went directly to Mr. van Pels, he came to see us immediately." (Anne Frank)

On July 5, 1942, thousands of Jews in the Netherlands, principally young Jewish refugees from Germany, receive a call-up notice to report for the *"werkverruiming"* ('work force project'). Among them are some youngsters who, just like the sixteen-year-old Margot Frank, receive a call-up on that Sunday afternoon. They will have to go without their parents. Late that afternoon Anne's friend Hello comes by again, but he is not allowed inside.

Margot and Anne are sent out of the room because Hermann van Pels wants to discuss the situation with Edith alone. Anne and Margot suspect then that they are going to go into hiding and they already begin to gather their things for packing. In her school satchel, Anne packs her diary, hair curlers, handkerchiefs, schoolbooks, a comb, and some old letters. At five o'clock, Otto Frank returns home. He was visiting an acquaintance at the Jewish Hospital. Otto and Edith decide to go directly into hiding the next day.

20 Anne Frank on the "balcony" (roof) of the house on Merwedeplein, circa 1940.
→ Already in the summer of 1941,

Otto Frank and the future helpers begin to furnish the hiding place on the Prinsengracht.

21

22

"So there we were walking though the pouring rain, Father, Mother and I, each of us with a school satchel and a shopping bag filled to the brim with the most varied assortment of items. The people on their way to work at that early hour gave us sympathetic looks; you could tell by their faces that they were sorry they couldn't offer us some kind of transportation; the conspicuous yellow star spoke for itself." (Anne Frank)

On Monday July 6th, Anne is awakened at five-thirty in the morning by her mother. It is less warm than Sunday, it rains throughout the day. In order to take as much as possible with them the family dresses in thick layers of clothing. Miep Gies comes along and takes Margot, on the bicycle, to the hiding place.

At seven-thirty, the rest of the family leaves the house on Merwedeplein and goes on foot to the Secret Annex located behind Otto Frank's company on the Prinsengracht. The house is left in such a state that it appears as if they have all fled in haste. One week later the Van Pels family – Hermann, Auguste and their son Peter – also comes to hide in the Secret Annex. On November 16, 1942, yet an eighth person joins all of them in hiding, Fritz Pfeffer. These eight people are taken care of by Otto Frank's most trusted employees: Miep Gies, Jo Kleiman, Victor Kugler and Bep Voskuijl. The people in hiding will spend more than two years in the Secret Annex.

21 Otto Frank's company on the
   Prinsengracht.
22 The hiding place, the annex
   of Otto Frank's company.

The People Who Go into Hiding

Otto Frank

Edith Frank-Holländer

Margot Frank

Anne Frank

Hermann van Pels

Auguste van Pels-Röttgen

Peter van Pels

Fritz Pfeffer

The Helpers

Miep Gies-Santrouschitz

Jo Kleiman

Victor Kugler

Bep Voskuijl

Going into Hiding

"We have to whisper and tread lightly during the day, otherwise the people in the warehouse might hear us." July 11, 1942

The Warehouse

1

2

The warehouse on the ground floor is run by several warehousemen supervised by the warehouse manager Johan Voskuijl, the father of the helper Bep Voskuijl, who herself works in the office. These workers grind the spices for Gies & Co and handle the distribution of Opekta goods. The office (staff) and warehouse (men) basically function independent of each other. Members of the office staff seldom go to the warehouse. Apart from Johan Voskuijl, the warehouse workers do not know anything about the hiding place. They are therefore a constant source of anxiety for those in hiding, just like the neighbors. When Johan Voskuijl becomes very ill, Willem van Maaren takes his place. All the inhabitants of the Secret Annex distrust Van Maaren.

1 The rear of the warehouse, where ground spices are weighed and packaged. Hermann van Pels is responsible for this part of the business. During the war there is a great demand for substitute spices. The trade in genuine spices, for the most part commodities originating from the then Netherlands East Indies, has come to a virtual standstill because of the war.

2 The pectin used in making jam and jelly is packaged in small packets and in bottles. Opekta also supplies membranes used for making an airtight

3

seal when preserving pots of jam. The firm distributes their products to drugstores and grocery stores and provides advice to housewives.

3 The Pectacon firm, which trades in spice and herb mixtures, is registered for the duration of the war and afterwards as Gies & Co., in the name of the non-Jewish helpers. Worked into the logo of the company is its location: by the tower of the Westerkerk, the church nearby. Special brand names are created for the various spice mixtures such as *EFWEKA* for the sausage spices.

4 The layout of the building on the Prinsengracht is so complicated that a new worker cannot readily discover the hiding place, especially since the warehousemen actually have no reason to go upstairs. The only warehouse employee advised of the situation is Johan Voskuijl, who falls ill in 1943 and is then no longer able to work. The warehouse personnel change repeatedly during the hiding period.

5 The front section of the warehouse with a bicycle cart used for deliveries of packaged spices and Opekta-articles.

5

4

6

6 The entry of the warehouse in the early 1950's with one of the warehousemen (unknown). During the war years, the large warehouse doors are
usually wide-open in the daytime. Consequently, the warehouse men
are witness to peculiar goings-on. Take for instance Lammert Hartog,
who starts working in the warehouse in the Spring of 1944. He notices
that the baker delivers a lot of bread and he discusses this with his wife
Lena, who cleans the building. The new warehouse manager Van Maaren
is also suspicious. He suspects that there are people in the building
at night.

*"Probably Van Maaren also has suspicions about us; he puts books and
bits of paper close to the edge of things in the warehouse so if anyone walks
by they fall off. Together with Kleiman, who just came by, Kugler and the
two gentlemen have been looking into the question of how to get rid of this
guy. Downstairs they think it's too risky. Yet isn't it even riskier to leave
things as they are?"* (April 25, 1944)

"Last night the four of us went down to the private office and listened to England on the radio. I was so scared that someone could hear us that I literally begged Father to go back upstairs with me; Mother understood my fear and went with me." July 11, 1942

The Private Office and the Kitchen

Once the personnel go home, those in hiding often come out of their hide-out. Then they go off to the office or other company spaces, or to the private office – Anne's name for the director's office. This office on the second floor, directly under the hiding place, is occasionally used for business meetings. Besides this, supplies are sometimes left there for the people in hiding. The kitchen is especially important for laundry. In the evenings and weekends the people in hiding can bathe, work, and listen to the radio in the private office. Sometimes they wash up in the kitchen and now and then Anne bathes in the lavatory. Warm water is hauled from the kitchen. Occasionally, Anne and Peter take a look outside by peeking through the curtains.

1 Jo Kleiman and A.W. Kwakernaak in the private office, 1954.
Anne writes that on two occasions Pomosin-Werke sales representatives
from Frankfurt come to discuss new Opekta deliveries. She notes on
April 1, 1943: *"The gentlemen arrived from Frankfurt and Father was already
nervous about the outcome of the meeting. 'If only I could be there, if only
I were downstairs,' he exclaimed. 'Go lie on the ground with your ear to the
floor, they'll be brought to the private office and then you can hear everything.' Father cheered up, and yesterday morning at ten-thirty Margot with
Pim (Father)—two ears are better than one—took up their posts on the floor."*

1

2

2 "I went downstairs all by myself and looked out through the windows of the private office and kitchen. I'm not imagining it when I say that looking up at the sky, the clouds, the moon, and the stars makes me feel calm and hopeful. It's better medicine than either valerian or bromide; nature makes me feel humble and ready to take each blow with courage. Just my luck that except for rare occasions, I'm only able to gaze at nature through very dirty windows with dusty curtains hanging in front of them." (June 13, 1944)

"Kugler, who at times finds the enormous responsibility for the eight of us overwhelming, can hardly talk from the pent-up tension and strain." May 26, 1944

Victor Kugler's Office

2   1

Prior to the hiding period, Victor Kugler shared this office with Hermann van Pels. During the hiding period Victor Kugler works here alone. He funnels money from the business to those in hiding and furthermore feels responsible for their safety. Kugler's office can only be reached via the front office and a door in the hallway, which can only be opened from the inside. Thus people entering from street level cannot simply walk directly through the hall to the staircase that leads to the hiding place. On the weekends and in the evenings the people in hiding, and Fritz Pfeffer in particular, use this office as a writing room.

1 Victor Kugler at his desk in 1941. He is primarily responsible for the spice department of the business. In the afternoons, he and the other helpers go and eat lunch with the people in hiding.

2 Each week Victor Kugler brings the people in hiding different magazines and newspapers like: *De Prins* (The Prince), *Het Rijk der Vrouw* (Women's World), *De Haagse Post* (The Hague Post), and sometimes the German publication *Das Reich* (The Third Reich). Anne especially looks forward to the magazine *Cinema & Theater*: *"Mr. Kugler makes me happy every Monday when he brings Cinema & Theater magazine along with him.*

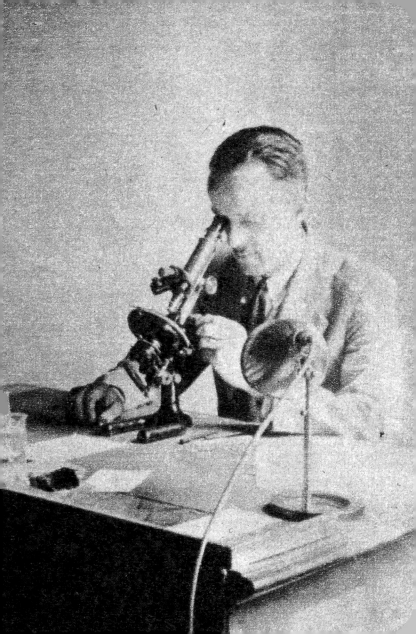

Though this small indulgence is often seen as a waste of money by the less worldly members of the household, they never fail to be amazed at how accurately I can name the actors in any given movie, even after a year."
(January 28, 1944)

"Our own helpers are still the best example; they've managed to pull us through so far. Never have they uttered a single word about the burden we must be."

January 28, 1944

The Front Office of Miep Gies, Jo Kleiman, and Bep Voskuijl

1

2

The front office is run by three people: Miep Gies, Jo Kleiman, and Bep Voskuijl. They are all indispensable for the assistance they provide to those in hiding. During the day the work must continue as normally as possible. The office personnel arrives at nine in the morning. The warehousemen downstairs have then been working since eight-thirty. In that half-hour the people in hiding must remain completely quiet. Not a sound must be detected. Once the office personnel arrives it becomes less of a problem. They know about what's happening, and the warehousemen can think that the noise originates from the office. Yet, those in hiding have to continually be as quiet as possible because traveling salesmen do come to the office. The helpers are also always on their guard. At five-thirty in the evening the helpers give the "all-clear" signal through to the Secret Annex. After hours and in the weekends those in hiding also use this front office.

1 On this machine Miep Gies types, for instance, letters for Opekta's "Helpful Hints" service. These include instructions about how to make jam using Opekta. Kugler also uses this typewriter for writing German business letters. In the evenings Otto Frank often takes the diverse typewriters up to the Secret Annex to prevent theft:

"Pim (Father) drags the typewriters upstairs," Anne reports on
August 10, 1943.

2 Otto Frank and the four helpers. From left to right: Miep Gies, Jo Kleiman,
Otto Frank, Victor Kugler, and Bep Voskuijl. The photo is taken after the
war, probably by Kugler using the camera's self-timer.

*"Every day all of them come upstairs and talk to the men about business
and politics, to the women about food and wartime difficulties, to the
children about books and newspapers. They manage to put on cheerful
faces, bring flowers and presents for birthdays and holidays, and are
always ready to do anything for us. That is what we should never forget,
that although others exhibit heroism in battle or by standing up to
the Germans, our helpers prove their heroism with their good spirits
and devotion."* (January 28, 1944)

3

4

3 The identity card of Jan Gies. The German occupier requires all residents
   of the Netherlands to carry an identity card with them at all times.
   The cards of Jews are stamped with a large letter *J*.

4 The identity card of Miep Gies-Santrouschitz.

5 Miep Gies does the daily grocery shopping together with Bep Voskuijl.
   She never knows what will be available: *"Every day the stores seemed
   emptier and the lines seemed longer."* What's more, Miep brings five
   library books along every Saturday and she keeps those in hiding abreast
   of the news from the outside world. Initially she relates everything about
   the razzias on the street, but when she realizes how disheartening this
   is to the inhabitants of the Secret Annex she keeps this information
   to herself.

"Miep has so much to carry she looks like a pack mule. She goes forth nearly every day to scrounge up vegetables, and then bicycles back with her purchases in large shopping bags. We always long for Saturdays, because then the books arrive. We're like little children receiving a present. Normal people simply don't know how much meaning books can have for people shut away. Reading, learning, and the radio are our only distractions." (July 11, 1943)

5

7

77

Handelsregister te Amsterdam van de Kamer van Koophandel en Fabrieken
voor NOORDHOLLAND

UITTREKSEL uit de opgaaf van __de naamlooze vennootschap: HANDELSVEREENIGING__
GIES & CO.N.V.₂ _____ gevestigd te__ AMSTERDAM.-C.,
Prinsengracht 263.

Ingeschreven onder No. 56645.

Als eenig directeur staat in de opgaaf vermeld:
VICTOR GUSTAV KUGLER, wonende te Hilversum, Emmasserweg 56,
Geboren te Hohenelbe (Dld.), 6 Juni 1900, nationaliteit: Nederlandsche.
Genaturaliseerd; 27 Mei 1938.

Aan
HANDELSVEREENIGING GIES & Co.N.V.,
Prinsengracht 263,
te _____ A M S T E R D A M.-C.

(Mod. 16e) (Uittreksel halffolio)

6

---

6 A certificate from the Trade Registry of the Chamber of Commerce.
From December 16, 1941, Otto Frank's companies are registered under
the names of the helpers.

7 Jo Kleiman's (on the left) recurring illness is a continuous worry.
In 1943 and 1944 he struggles with his stomach. When he's feeling better,
he comes to the office as much as possible. *"Luckily Mr. Kleiman is
around,"* Anne frequently writes with relief in her diary. No matter the
situation, Jo Kleiman is the person that the people in hiding can always
count on. He and is brother even help during the preparations for going
into hiding. Otto Frank discusses all business affairs with him. Kleiman
keeps in contact with Opekta's license holder in Basel--Erich Elias, the
brother-in-law of Otto and Edith Frank. By calamities such as break-ins,
a flea infestation, or an unexpected visitor, Kleiman is the first one to size
up the situation. Also, according to Anne: *"he is a fantastic source of the
latest citywide gossip."*

8

8 Bep Voskuijl's identity card. Bep initially goes to work as a domestic and in a sewing workshop. She follows various evening courses to become a fully-qualified office-clerk. This profession is one of the few good professional opportunities for young women from blue-collar and middle-class families. It is considered schooled work and pays decently.

9 Bep Voskuijl (left), with her office colleages, Miep, Esther, and Pine in front of the building on the Prinsengracht, 1941. Bep, together with Miep Gies, is responsible for the food provisions. She is the oldest child of a family with six children. Her full name is Elisabeth, but mostly she is called Bep. Because there isn't enough for everyone to eat at home she eats her daily meal with those in hiding. Just like Miep and Jan, Bep also spends a night (October 30, 1942) in the Secret Annex. At home the Voskuijl family does not discuss the people in hiding, still both the father and also sister Corry help out. Father Voskuijl builds the bookcase and Corry, a seamstress, makes clothing for Anne and Margot.

"Bep almost had a nervous breakdown this week because she had to do so many errands. Ten times a day people were sending her out for something, each time insisting that she go right away or go again or that she'd done it

wrong. If you just think that she still has to finish her office work downstairs, that Kleiman is ill, Miep is at home with a cold, and that Bep herself has a sprained ankle, boyfriend troubles, and a grumpy father at home, then it's no wonder that she's at her wits end." (September 29,1943)

9

Evenings and in the weekends, when the business is closed down, the people in hiding often come out of the hiding place. Sometimes they come to the front office, where the thick curtains are drawn closed after business hours. For Anne, who is dying for a glimpse of the outside world, this is a thrilling room.

"I'm sitting cozily in the front office looking outside through a chink in the heavy curtains. It's dusk, but still just light enough to write. It's really strange watching people walking by, it seems as if they're all in a terrible hurry and are practically tripping over their own feet. The bicycles whiz by so fast that I can't even tell what sort of person is riding the thing."
(December 13, 1942)

"The people in this neighborhood aren't so very attractive and the children in particular are so dirty you wouldn't want to touch them with a ten-foot pole—real slum kids with runny noses. I can hardly understand a word they say. Yesterday afternoon Margot and I were taking a bath here and I said: 'If we took a fishing rod and reeled in each of those kids one by one as they walked by, put them in a bath, washed and mended their clothes, and then let them go again, then…' To this Margot replied: 'And then tomorrow, they'd be just as filthy and look just as ragged as before.'"
(December 13, 1942)

"As if I'd seen one of the World Wonders, I saw two Jews through the curtain yesterday, it was a horrible feeling, just as if I had betrayed them to the authorities and was now watching them in their misery."
(December 13, 1942)

"Countless friends and acquaintances have been taken off to a dreadful fate. Night after night, green and gray military vehicles cruise the streets. It's impossible to escape their clutches unless you go into hiding." November 19, 1942

The Storeroom

1

The third floor of the front part of the house is used for storage during
the war years. The spices are stockpiled in the rear of the space.
To protect them from the light the windows are covered over with blue
paint. This also keeps the hiding place from being discovered by out-
siders who might come to this floor.
Anne Frank hears the news about the ongoing persecution of the
Jews from the helpers, the radio, and Fritz Pfeffer--a later arrival to the
Secret Annex. She describes these accounts in her diary. Step-by-step,
Nazi-Germany forces the Jews of Europe into a corner. Under the guise
of "labor camps", the Nazis deport large numbers of Jews "to the East".
The exact destination is kept secret, just like the true nature of these
so-called labor camps.

1 The storeroom in 1954. During the war years Opekta's mixing barrels
   are kept here. All sorts of packing goods and raw materials are also
   stored here. The people in hiding basically never come here, not even
   in the evenings.

2 One of the few photos made of a razzia in Amsterdam. It is early in
   the morning on May 26, 1943. The center of Amsterdam is surrounded.

85

Three thousand Jews are removed from their homes. They are taken by train to Westerbork and from there to one of the extermination camps. The pharmacist on Geldersekade made this photograph of his neighbors being led away.

2

3

4

5

3 Apprehended Jews awaiting transport to Westerbork, 1942.
Massive razzias occur throughout the Netherlands on the 2nd and 3rd
of October 1942. By the end of 1942, 40,000 of the Jews living in the
Netherlands have been deported.

4 Amsterdam, April 1943. This streetcar is taking Jews to Muiderpoort
train station. From there they will be deported further, to Westerbork
transit camp. An armed German soldier is standing on the footboard.
Transports are usually carried out early in the morning, yet many
bystanders still witness the deportations. In Amsterdam the last mass
razzias occur in 1943, on June 20th and September 29th. Of the 140,000
Jews in the Netherlands, 107,000 are deported. Only 5,000 of them will
survive the camps.

5 A small percentage of Jews succeeds in evading arrest and deportation
by means of, for example, taking on a different identity. These people are
given or sold forged identity cards by the Resistance. This organization's
reach and resolve against the German occupying force increases as the
war progresses.

6

6 In 1948, Victor Kugler testifies that he once came across Van Maaren, the warehouseman, in the storeroom: *"To block the view of the so-called Secret Annex we had daubed several windows in the rear of the front part of the house with blue paint, supposedly for blackout purposes. On one particular occasion I caught Van Maaren in the act of scratching away some of the blue paint on a window and he reacted by saying: 'Hey, I've never been over there.'"*

← It appears from Anne's diary that this storage space was not only used for spices and other company articles, but also for storing food for the people in hiding: *"Besides, we still have about 230 pounds of winter potatoes in the rear of the spice storeroom."* (February 3, 1944)

"Now our Secret Annex has truly become secret.
Mr. Kugler thought it would be better have
a bookcase built in front of the entrance."

August 21, 1942

The Movable Bookcase

Once the Frank family and the Van Pels family have been in hiding for more than a month, a decision is made to camouflage the entry door to the Annex. To do this, the stoop leading up to the Annex's gray door needs to be removed and then the door itself can be lowered. The warehouse manager Voskuijl builds the movable bookcase. The short staircase opening onto the landing in front of the bookcase leads down to the office spaces on the second floor. The helpers use this stairway when they visit the Secret Annex. In the evenings and on weekends, when the people in hiding come out of the Secret Annex, they descend this staircase to get to the offices below.

On July 6, 1942, when the people in hiding first arrive at the Annex there is just an ordinary door on this spot. You enter the Annex by way of a few steps. Anne writes: *"No one would ever suspect that there could be so many rooms hidden behind that plain gray-painted door. There's just a small stoop going up to the door, and then you're inside. (July 9, 1942)* Victor Kugler hits on the idea of making a movable bookcase to conceal the entranceway.

"Mr. Voskuijl has finished building the contraption; before doing that the walls of the landing had to be papered. Now whenever we want to go downstairs we have to duck and then jump. After three days we were all walking around with foreheads full of lumps from bumping our heads against the lowered doorway. Then Peter made it as soft as possible by nailing a piece of cloth filled with wood-wool to it. Let's see if that helps!" (August 21, 1942)

1 Due to the removal of two treads one has to take a step of more than $1\frac{1}{2}$ feet to enter the Annex. A panel is used to board-up the opening at the top of the doorway.

95

1

A wooden staircase ascends from the floor where the offices are located to the landing in front of the movable bookcase. The helpers use this staircase when they want to go to the Secret Annex. *"Kugler comes up the stairs hurry-scurry, a short sturdy knock on the door and in he comes, wringing his hands in proportion to his mood, either good-tempered and boisterous or bad tempered and silent."* (August 5, 1943)

← Today, the stairwell is sealed-off with a piece of glass.

"It was just after five on Friday afternoon. I came out of my room and was about to sit down at the table to write when I was roughly pushed aside to make room for Margot and Father, who wanted to practice their Latin." November 11, 1943

Otto, Edith and Margot Frank's Room

Today the rooms of the Annex are empty. The furniture and remaining belongings of the people in hiding are carted away, by order of the German occupier, shortly after the arrest. In this space, the sitting-room of the Frank family, pencil marks recording the height of Anne and Margot and a map of Normandy can still be seen on the wall. The Frank family spends the major portion of the day here during the hiding period. After the arrival of Fritz Pfeffer, Margot sleeps in this room with her parents. Sometimes the tensions among the family members run high, yet there are also always reoccurrences of harmony.

1

1 *"Margot Frank is learning: English and French; Latin via a correspondence course; shorthand in English, German and Dutch; mechanics; goniometry; stereometry; physics; chemistry; algebra; geometry; English, French, German and Dutch literature; bookkeeping; geography; modern history; biology; economics; reads everything, preferably about religion and medicine."* (May 16, 1944)

→ Probably the last photo taken of Margot and Anne.

→ From the moment they go into hiding, Otto and Edith keep track of how much their daughters grow. In those two years Anne grows more than five inches and Margot around two inches.

2 Using her own name, Bep Voskuijl orders a Latin correspondence course for Margot. The teacher has no idea that a Jewish girl in hiding is doing the course. Anne says regarding this: *"Margot sends her Latin lessons to a teacher, who corrects and then returns them. She's registered under Bep's name. The teacher's very nice, and witty too. I bet he's glad to have such a smart student."* (November 17, 1943)

2

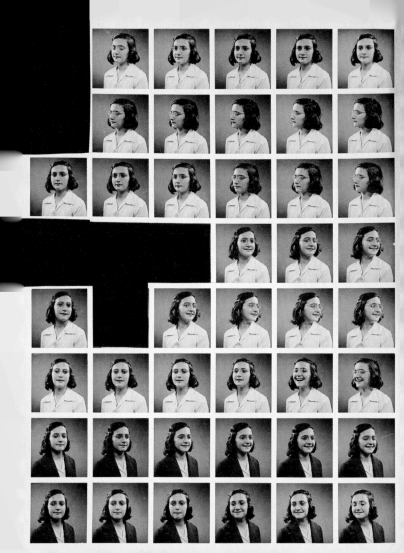

3   4

3   During the hiding period, Edith Frank keeps the various rooms in the Annex clean and does the dishes. In addition, she reads a lot and just like Margot, takes a correspondence course. Anne writes in her diary: *"Mrs. Frank: learns English by correspondence course; reads everything except detective stories."* (May 16, 1944)

4   Edith Frank is a religious woman. She tries to pass this on to her daughters but with no success, as Anne herself indicates: *"Father has taken the plays of Goethe and Schiller down from the big bookcase and is planning to read to me every evening. We've already started Don Carlos. Encouraged by Father's good example, Mother pressed her prayer book into my hands. I read a few prayers in German, just to be polite. They certainly sound beautiful, but don't mean very much to me. Why is she always pushing me to behave so saintly and devout?"* (October 29, 1942)

108

5 Edith Frank finds being in hiding very difficult. She does not get along
with the Van Pels family and is pessimistic about the future. In spite of
her gloominess she still makes plans for after the war. According to
Miep Gies, Edith, just like her eldest daughter, wanted to go to Palestine.
In the eyes of her youngest daughter, Edith cannot do much of anything
right. Anne sees her only as an example of how not to do things.

5

→ Anne Frank admires her father and is simply crazy about him. She gives him the pet name Pim. *"I love them, but only because they're Mother and Margot, as people they can go fly a kite. It's different with Father. When I see him being partial to Margot, approving Margot's every action, praising and hugging her, I feel a gnawing ache inside, because I'm crazy about him. He's the only one I look up to, in the entire world I don't love anyone but Father."* (November 7, 1942) Later Anne's opinion of her father shifts and she distances herself much more.

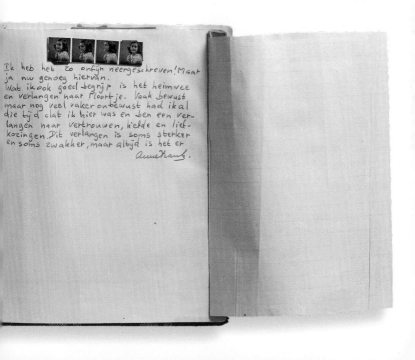

in mijn dagboek schrijven. Mev. Kleiman en Kleijn en ook Bep Voskuyl hebben ons zo geholpen, we hebben al rabarber aardbeien en kersen gehad, en ik dink niet, dat we ons hier voorlopig zullen vervelen. van Pels verteld het praatje dat papa bevriend is met een kapitein uit het leger en die heeft hem geholpen om naar België te komen. die praatje weet nu iedereen en wij vermaken ons erover. Te lezen hebben we ook en we kopen nog een hele hoop spelletjes.

Uit het raam kijken of naar buiten gaan mogen wij natuurlijk nooit Ook moeten we zachtjes zijn, want be- reden mogen ze ons niet horen.

Nu houd ik op want ik heb nog veel te doen.

het verhaal wordt ernstiger, maar een glimlach is er nog over van het grappige gedeelte.
oh wat een mop.
- wat zou er nou komen?

← ook lief

↑ ddàg; "Jamij gaat het goed!" (lachende beleefdheid.)

↑ het verhaal is leuk

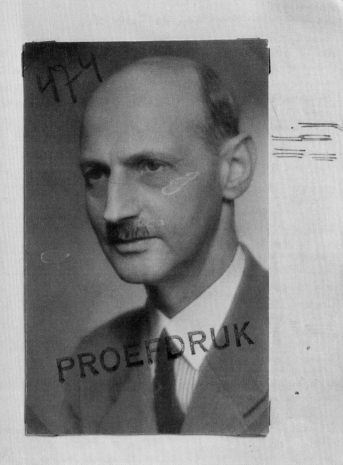

PROEFDRUK

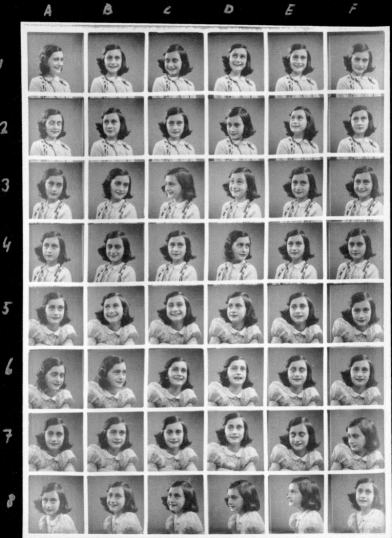

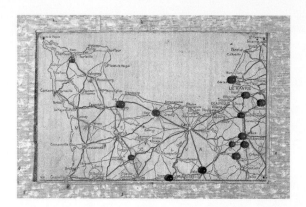

6

6 On June 6, 1944, the Allied Forces land in Normandy. Otto Frank keeps track of the progress of the Allied invasion on a small map he's cut out of the daily newspaper *De Telegraaf* (The Telegraph). Every day the people in hiding follow the advance of the Allied Forces on the radio. Anne writes: *"'This is D-day,' the English radio said at twelve o'clock and rightly so! 'This is the day,' came the announcement over the English news at twelve o'clock. The invasion has begun!* (June 6, 1944)

"Great commotion in the Annex! Is this really the beginning of the long-awaited liberation? The liberation about which so much has been said, but which seems too wonderful, too much like a fairy tale, ever to come true? Will this year, 1944, bring us victory? We don't know yet, but where there's hope, there's life, and this restores our courage and makes us strong again. Margot says that maybe I can even go back to school in October or September." (June 6, 1944)

"Yet, what's nicest of all is that at least I can still write down my thoughts and feelings, otherwise I'd just totally suffocate." March 15, 1944

Anne Frank and Fritz Pfeffer's Room

Anne and Margot sleep together in this room for a number of months. Fritz Pfeffer, the new person in hiding, moves in with Anne in November 1942 and then Margot goes to her parents' room. Anne is initially positive about her new roommate, but that quickly changes and she writes about him in a very negative manner. Both of them prefer to be alone in the small room when writing, reading, or working. This causes a great deal of strife. Only once she's lying in bed at night does Anne have the peace and quiet to think about herself, the others, the dangers of the outside world, and about day-to-day occurrences. Hope and fear, low-spirits, the desire to live, falling in love, cheerfulness; Anne writes about all these emotions in her diary.

1 Anne glues prints from her collection to the two blank walls of her small room. These images give us an impression of her broad range of interests, for example: film stars, nature, history and royalty. Leonardo da Vinci and Rembrandt alongside Greta Garbo and Ginger Rogers.

"Our little room looked very bare at first with nothing on the walls; but thanks to Daddy who had brought my film-star collection on beforehand, and with the aid of a paste pot and brush, I have transformed the walls into one gigantic picture. This makes it look much more cheerful." (July 11, 1942)

Anne misses her girlfriends, school, her cat Mouschi, and is very aware of the constant danger. Jews who have gone into hiding are threatened with severe punishments. *"Not being able to go outside upsets me more than I can say, and I'm terrified that we will be discovered and that we'll be shot."* (September 28, 1942)

"I spend many Sundays sorting through my large collection of film stars, which has reached quite a respectable size by now." (January 28, 1944)

2

3

2 Heinz Rühmann. A still from the German movie *Paradies der Junggesellen*.

3 Greta Garbo in the film *Ninotchka*, 1939.

4 Ginger Rogers.

5 Anne often fantasizes about being an actress in the United States. She also writes a short story about this entitled: "Dreams of Movie Stardom", in response to *"the questions of Mrs. van Pels who never tires of asking me why I wouldn't want to become a movie star."* In the story Anne imagines herself as a seventeen-year-old girl who ends up in Hollywood as the guest of a famous film star. But it's not at all what she expects and she writes: *"As for dreams of movie stardom, I was cured."* (Anne's Storybook, December 24, 1943)

→ *"This is a photograph of me as I wish I looked all the time. Then I might still have a chance of getting to Hollywood. But at present, I'm afraid I usually look quite different."* (October 18, 1942)

4   5

Anne has a great many hobbies and interests. She elaborates on these in her diary entry of April 6, 1944: *"First of all: writing, but I don't really think of that as a hobby."* She further lists tracking down family trees of royal families. *"So my third hobby is history, and Father's already bought me numerous books."*

16. Oct. 1942.
Vrijdag

Beste Jet,

Als Emmy een krabbel ertussen door krijgt, heb jij ook geen stiefbrief. dus hoe gaat er me. Alweer een beetje vande schrik bekomen, ik hoop van wel. Hier is gelukkig nog alles bij het oude. Ik heb vandaag 9 bladen gemaakt van de Franse onregelmatige werbw. Het is een precies en vervelend werkje maar ik wil het graag afmaken. Ik heb nog niets aan Henri gehoord mis- schien Maandavond nog. maar het is Vrij dag dus dat is critisch. Mama is weer bij een rotbui. We hebben gehoord dat de familie Stokvisch is gaan schuilen, gelukt weg maar. Ik ben nu Körner aan het lezen, die schrijft erg leuk. Nu tot de volgende keer. Gedag - liefs van

Anne Frank

anzo in 't een spiegel

Ho kijk ik ← in een kinder- wagen

Dit is ← ook snoezig hé.

Anne.

Hier heb ik zeker naar de harlekijn gekeken.
Anne

10 Oct. 1942
Zontg.

Lieve Marianne,   10 Oct.
                         Zon.
gisteren is het schrijven er weer bij ingeschoten. En eerste omdat ik de lijst va Franse werkwoorden af maken en ten twed omdat ik ook nog ander werk had. Ik heb weer 2 boeken van Kleiman kregen, De Arcadia. Dat de over een reis naar

een ontsettende tuchtsprong. later wolten
en grappen over hoe de lessen zijn.
2e deel. Anne met vrite en op school.
In het kamertje met Kitty en twee jongens
waaronder Bernd aan theetafel bezig
dan op school onveilig door een storm
van kinderen en allerlei diverse toneelen
b.v. in bed met Peder en aan tafel.
3e deel Anne haar toiletten de Parisien
...spelen geschenk als cadeau ...
witte en sehoenen.

bergen en De Louteringskuur, ze lijken me wel leuk.
De Opstandelingen heeft ze ook mee gebracht. Dat
is van Ammers Küller. Dezelfde schrijfster als van
Heeren, Vrouwen, Knechten. Dit mag ik nu ook lezen, fijn!
Dan heb ik een hele boel liefde's romantoneelstukjes
van körner gelezen, ik vind dat die man leuk schrijft.
B.v. Hedwig, der
Vetter aus Brehem,
tons Heilings Felsen,
Der Grüne, Domino,
Die Gouvernante,
Der Vierjährige
Posten. Die Sühne,
Der kampf mit dem
Drachen, Der Nacht-
wächter en zoal
meer. Vader wil dat
ik nu ook Hebbel en
andere boeken van
andere welbekende
Duitse schrijvers
ga lezen. Het Duits
lezen, gaat nu al be-
vrekkelijk vlot. Alleen
luister ik het meestal, in plaats dat ik voor
mezelf lees. Maar dat gaat wel over. Gisteren heb

Dit is een
foto, zoals
ik me zou
wensen,
altijd zo
te zijn.
Dan had
ik nog wel een kans
om naar Holywood te
komen. Maar tegen-
woordig zie ik er
jammer genoeg mees-
tal anders uit.
Anne Frank,
10 Oct. 1942.
Zondag.

ik veel wat
filmsterren
in de kamer
opgehangen
maar nu
met foto-
hoekjes, dan
kan ik ze
er weer af-
halen. Ben
ik gisteren
naar de
baad ge-
gaan en
heeft Ekken
ken voor
Margot en
mij gekocht.
Maar ze
moeten weer
geruild, want
ze passen
niet hele-
maal.

6

7

6 Self-portrait of Leonardo da Vinci.

7 Detail of Michelangelo's *Pietà*.

8 Rembrandt: *Portrait of an Old Man*.

9 A picture postcard showing members of the Dutch Royal family, who lived in exile in Canada during the war. In the Netherlands the postcard is distributed by the illegal Resistance newspaper *Trouw* ('Loyalty'). *"Bep has had a picture postcard of the entire Royal Family made for me. Juliana looks very young, and so does the Queen. The three little girls are adorable. It was incredibly nice of Bep, don't you think?"* (December 30, 1943)

10 Right from the very beginning of the hiding period, Margot, Anne and Peter keep up with their schoolwork. They are hopeful that the war will quickly come to an end and they don't want to have fallen behind in school. Otto Frank makes sure that they do their lessons correctly and helps them when necessary. On April 6, 1944 Anne complains: *"I loathe algebra, geometry, and arithmetic. I enjoy all my other school subjects, but history's my favorite."*

8

9

10

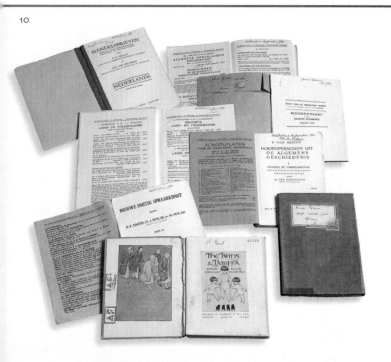

De eerste film van Deanna Durbin in
haar nieuwste film , Firat Love'.
Zij is thans acteerin tien en veelges
Amerikaansche begrijpen mensig
nadat zij thans een kinderbilm mor
speelt, doch fielde gaat heeltren maar
om jongenen. Dat is Robert Stock,
een bal middelste filmbepaking, dan
een klet is een buitenni met Deanna
itili algeheld.

H.R.H. THE PRINCESS ELIZABETH OF YORK

TROUW

H.R.H. THE PRINCESS MARGARET ROSE OF YORK

NORMA SHEARER

POLDERLANDSCHAP
LANGS DE EEM BIJ BAARN

132

15/XI. 1942.   Amsterdam - Zuid

Meine einzige Innigstgeliebte!

Du sollst einen Morgengruß von mir erhalten.
Mir fällt es diesmal so schwer dir zu schreiben,
da wir Alles täglich besprechen konnten.
Und doch freibt euch mein Herz dran, da es
so voll Stolz für Dich, meine von Herzen Geliebte,
ist. Ich bewunderte alle Zeit deine so tapfere,
stille Größe und deinen Adel, mit denen du
diese unbeschreiblich schwere Tat meisterst.
Mein Stolz besteht in meiner ganzen Hingabe
für Dich, in meinem Streben, Tun und Lassen,
mich deiner Liebe würdig zu zeigen.
Was bedeutet diese hoffentlich fast kurze Unterbrechung
in dem ewig unzerreißbaren Band!
Halte weiter deinen herrlichen Mut, dein Gottvertrauen
und unsere Liebe wird auch uns stärken und
tapfer halten. In diesem Sinne umarmt und
              küßt Dich innigst   Dein Fritz

Von diesen Zigaretten, die ich so
lange für dich bewahrte, rauche täglich mir eine.

2   1

Fritz Pfeffer is Miep Gies' dentist and also knows the Frank family well. He asks Miep if she knows of a place to hide. The inhabitants of the Secret Annex agree to his joining them. Anne is even enthusiastic: *"Great news! We're planning to take an eighth person into hiding with us!"* (November 10, 1942) Pfeffer is very surprised to see the Frank Family again on November 16, 1942, because he thought they had left for Switzerland. Anne now shares her small room with Pfeffer.

1 Charlotte Kaletta and Fritz Pfeffer around 1940.

2 Fritz Pfeffer writes, in a farewell letter to Charlotte Kaletta, on November 15, 1942: *"My dearly beloved wife, what can this, hopefully short separation possibly mean compared to our eternal bond? Hold onto your magnificent courage and your trust in God, and your love will make me and us strong and courageous"*. In the months that follow, Pfeffer writes letters to her on a regular basis. Miep Gies acts as *postillion d'amour* ('courier of love'), but his place of hiding remains a secret.

3

4

3 Anne prefers to work at her small desk when writing, reading and studying. But Pfeffer also puts claims on the small table. Anne asks him *"whether he would please be so good as to allow me (see how polite I am?) to use the table in our room two afternoons a week, from four to five-thirty. I already sit there every day from two-thirty to four when Pfeffer takes a nap, but the rest of the time the room and the table are off-limits to me."* (July, 13, 1943) Yet, Pfeffer refuses by saying that anyway Anne is not seriously busy.

4 In her diary Anne makes a short list of the activities of the people in hiding. She says concerning Fritz Pfeffer: *"Learns English, Spanish, and Dutch, without noticeable results. Reads everything, agrees with the majority."* (May 16, 1944) Fritz Pfeffer is studying Spanish because he plans to emigrate to South America with Charlotte Kaletta after the war. In his Spanish textbook Actividades Comerciales ('Commercial Activities') he makes this notation: *"25.VII. 44 1½ de la tarde achterhuis"*. (July 25, 1944, 1:30 in the afternoon, annex).

5 Anne runs to her father, who also ends up having a discussion with Fritz Pfeffer. *"And so the conversation went back and forth, with Father defending*

my 'selfishness' and my 'busywork' and Pfeffer grumbling the whole time. Pfeffer finally had to give in and I was granted the opportunity to work without interruption two afternoons a week. Pfeffer looked very sullen, didn't speak to me for two days and made sure he occupied the table from five to five-thirty—all very childish, of course. A person of fifty-four who is still so pedantic and small-minded must be so by nature, and will never improve." (July 13 1943)

6 Tuesday, March 28, 1944 is an important day for Anne.

"Mr. Bolkestein, the Cabinet Minister, speaking on the Dutch broadcast from London, said that after the war, a collection would be made of diaries and letters dealing with the war. Of course everyone pounced on my diary. Just imagine how interesting it would be if I were to publish a novel about the Secret Annex. The title alone would make people think it was a detective story." (March 29, 1944) Anne decides to edit her diary notes so she can publish them later on. *"But, and that's a big question, will I ever be able to write something great, will I ever become a journalist or a writer? I hope so, oh I hope so very much, because writing allows me to record everything, all my thoughts, ideals and fantasies."* (April 5, 1944)

6

138

7 Sometimes Anne has serious doubts about her end result.
"My writing's all mixed up, I'm jumping from one thing to another and sometimes I seriously doubt whether anyone will ever be interested in this drivel. They'll probably call it 'The Musings of an Ugly Duckling'."
(April 14, 1944)

7

When she's lying in bed in the evenings and in the middle of the night, Anne has the time and space to think about herself and others.

"Oh well, so much comes into my head at night when I'm alone, or during the day when I'm obliged to put up with people I can't abide or who invariably misinterpret my intentions. That's why I always wind up coming back to my diary – I start there and end there because Kitty's always patient. I promise her that, despite everything, I'll keep on going. I'll pave my own way and I'll swallow my tears." (November 7, 1942)

Anne frequently wakes-up in the middle of the night and then she listens to the nightly sounds.

"In the first place, to hear if there are any burglars downstairs, and then to the various beds—upstairs, next door and in my room – to tell whether the others are asleep or half awake. This is no fun, especially when it concerns a member of the family named Dr. Pfeffer. First there's the sound of a fish gasping for air, and this is repeated nine or ten times. Then the lips are moistened profusely. This is alternated with little smacking sounds, followed by a long period of tossing and turning and rearranging the pillows." (August 4, 1943)

Sometimes Anne despairs.

"At night in bed I see myself alone in a dungeon, without Father and Mother. Or I'm roaming the streets, or the Annex is on fire, or they come in the middle of the night to take us away and I crawl under my bed in desperation. I see everything as if it were actually taking place. And to think it might all happen soon! I simply can't imagine the world will ever be normal again for us." (November 8, 1943)

Anne desperately yearns for the open air.

"Whenever someone comes in from outside, with the wind in their clothes and the cold on their cheeks, I feel like burying my head under the blankets to keep from thinking: 'When will we be allowed to breathe fresh air again?' And because I'm not allowed to do that – on the contrary, I have to hold my head up high and put a bold face on things, but the thoughts keep coming anyway. Not just once, but over and over, countless times. Believe me, if you've been shut up for a year and a half, it sometimes gets to be too much. But feelings can't be ignored, no matter how unjust or ungrateful they seem. I long to ride a bike, dance, whistle, look at the world, feel young and know that I'm free." (December 24, 1943)

"Margot and Mother are nervous. 'Shh... Father, be quiet, Otto, ssh...Come here, you can't run the water any more. Walk softly!' A sample of what's said to Father in the bathroom." August 23, 1943

The Bathroom

Eight people having access to only one toilet and sink means that those in hiding often have to wait their turn. The additional problem exists that the facilities cannot be used too often, because the sound of streaming water could give them away. For instance, the toilet may be flushed in the daytime during office hours, but not too frequently. It can definitely be heard in the warehouse, but the workers there do not suspect that anyone else other than the office employees could be responsible for the sound. The toilet is also a place for the people in hiding to retreat to, to find some privacy in the crowded Secret Annex.

1

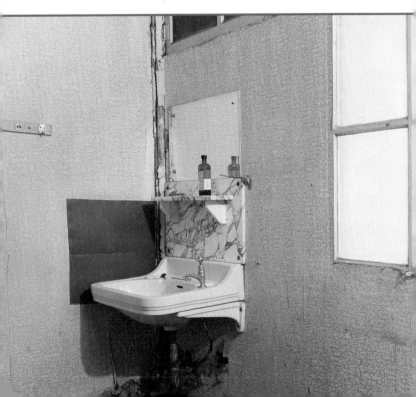

145

2

1 Fritz Pfeffer often goes to the toilet so he can be alone for a moment. Anne characterizes him as follows: *"Pants that come up to his chest, a red jacket, black patent-leather slippers and horn-rimmed glasses – that's how he looks when he's at work at the little table, always studying and never progressing. This is interrupted only by his afternoon nap, food and – his favorite spot – the bathroom. Three, four or five times a day there's bound to be someone waiting outside the bathroom door, hopping impatiently from one foot to another, trying to hold it in and barely managing. Does Pfeffer care? Not a whit."* (August 9, 1943)

Yet, Anne often has the need to be alone for just a moment too. *"Suddenly I felt the tears coming again. I raced downstairs to the bathroom, grabbing the hand mirror on the way. I sat there on the toilet, fully dressed, long after I was through, my tears leaving dark spots on the red of my apron, and I felt utterly wretched."* (February 19, 1944)

2 Anne continues to be annoyed with the toilet behavior of Pfeffer. *"This afternoon I boldly took a piece of pink paper and wrote: Mr. Pfeffer's Toilet Timetable Mornings from 7:15 - 7:30 A.M.*

Afternoons after 1:00 P.M.
Otherwise, only as needed!

I tacked this to the green bathroom door while he was still inside.
I might well have added: Transgressors will be subject to confinement!
Because our bathroom can be locked from both the inside and the
outside." (May 9, 1944)

"Nine o'clock, Sunday evening. The teapot, under its cozy, is on the table, and the guests enter the room. Pfeffer sits to the left of the radio, Mr. v.P. in front of it and Peter to the side. Mother is next to Mr. v.P., with Mrs. v.P. behind them. Margot and I are sitting in the last row and Pim at the table." March 27, 1944

Hermann and Auguste van Pels' Room

1

On the top floor of the Secret Annex is Hermann and Auguste van Pels' room, which at the same time functions as the common living room. Around noontime, the helpers from the office and Jan Gies come to eat lunch here. In the evening all eight people in hiding and the helper Bep Voskuijl eat at the large table in this room. Now and then, Mr. and Mrs. Kleiman visit on the weekend. Mr. and Mrs. van Pels therefore have even less privacy than the Frank family. The joint meals offer companionship, but also give rise to conflicts, for instance, about upbringing. "To not fancy some kind of food" is inconceivable for the Van Pelses, while Anne finds this very normal. As time passes being in hiding becomes more difficult. Not only do supplies shrink, tensions also increase.

1 Upon their arrival at the Secret Annex on July 13, 1942, 'Mr. v.P.' and 'Mrs. v.P.' (or Madam) – as Anne usually refers to the Van Pelses – bring along a few unusual personal objects. *"Mrs. v.P. was carrying a hatbox with a large potty inside. 'I just don't feel at home without my chamber pot,' she exclaimed, and it was the first item to find a permanent place under the divan. Instead of a chamber pot, Mr. v.P. was lugging a collapsible tea table under his arm. From the first, we ate our meals together, and after three days it felt as if the seven of us had become one big family."* (August 14, 1942)

"Some people, seem to take special delight in raising not only their own children but in helping others raise theirs, for instance v.P.'s. You should hear us at mealtimes, with reprimands and saucy replies flying to and fro. If I take a small helping of some vegetable I detest and eat potatoes instead, the v.P.'s, and Madam in particular, can't get over how spoiled I am. 'Come on, Anne, eat some more vegetables,' she says." (September 27, 1942)

2 In this room, all the people in hiding gather for preparing and eating meals and at anxious moments. Even though everyone takes part in the housekeeping chores, this sometimes still leads to quarreling. One of Anne's "short stories" is devoted to this: *"The Battle of the Potatoes"* (August 4, 1943). According to Hermann van Pels, Anne and Margot would *"be better off, if they helped out more instead of always having their noses in a book, it isn't necessary for girls to learn so much!"* Edith Frank does not agree with this at all and *"therefore it doesn't happen"*.

2

3

3 Hermann van Pels loves good food, likes to crack a joke and is usually in a bad mood when there's a shortage of cigarettes. He has an outspoken opinion about politics and willingly speculates about the duration of the war. In contrast to the other Secret Annex occupants, he does not follow any study courses. He enjoys looking things up in the encyclopedia and reads preferably *"detective stories, medical books and love stories, exciting and trivial,"* as Anne describes it. While in hiding he works for Otto's business. In the evening he regularly goes to the warehouse where the spice mixtures are made. (May 16, 1944)

"Usually joins in the conversation, never fails to give his opinion. Once he's spoken, his word is final. If anyone dares to suggest otherwise, he can put up a good fight. Oh...he can hiss like a cat... but I'd rather he didn't... Once you've seen it, you never want to see it again. His opinion is the best, he knows the most about everything. Granted, the man has a good head on his shoulders, but it's swelled to no small degree." (August 9, 1943)

4 Hermann van Pels makes this shopping list for Miep Gies. *"To Credit: Three coupons,"* so it says, *"two for the liver-sausage and one for the blood-sausage."* The list for the order continues: *"One and a half blood-sausage, one blood-sausage and one and a half liver-sausage. Calf legs or a small calf's head."* Hermann van Pels has many contacts in the butcher's branch who deliver extra meat without ration coupons. As early as the spring of 1942, he takes Miep Gies along with him to a sympathetic butcher in the neighborhood. At first Miep does not understand why. Later, this butcher helps Miep when she comes to do the shopping for the people in hiding.

4

5

"Mr. van Pels used to be in the meat, sausage, and spice business.
We ordered a large amount of meat (under the counter, of course)
which we were planning to preserve in case there were hard times ahead.
He proposed making frying sausages, Gelderland sausages and sausage
spread. It was such a comical sight. The room was in a glorious mess:
Mr. v.P., clad in his wife's apron and looking fatter than ever, was working
away at the meat. What with his bloody hands, red face and spotted apron,
he looked like a real butcher." (December 10, 1942)

5 Auguste van Pels is the "hard-working housewife" and the chief cook of
the Secret Annex. Anne's opinion about "Madam" changes repeatedly,
and she can write volumes about her. Sometimes Anne can have a good
conversation with her, the next moment she finds her unbearable and
pretentious and then once again cheerful, industrious and tidy. Auguste
likes to read biographies and novels. She learns English by correspondence course. She occupies herself further with knitting, cooking, doing
the wash, and if we are to believe Anne, complaining and causing trouble.
She also exercises.

LEHRBÜCHER

METHODE GASPEY-OTTO-SAUER

VALETTE
KLEINE
NIEDERLÄNDISCHE
SPRACHLEHRE

JULIUS GROOS, HEIDELBERG

6

7

"Smile coquettishly, pretend you know everything, offer everyone a piece of advice and mother them – that's sure to make a good impression. But if you take a better look, the good impression fades. One, she's hard working; two, cheerful; three, coquettish – and sometimes a cute face. That's Gusti van Pels." (August 9, 1943)

6   While in hiding, Auguste van Pels, or Gusti, attempts to learn Dutch. *"Mrs. van Pels was trying to do everything at once: learning Dutch out of a book, stirring the soup, watching the meat, sighing and moaning about her broken rib."* (December 10, 1942) Anne comments a lot about the Dutch of "Madam", as well as that of her mother. *"That irritated Mrs. v.P., who continued her story with a string of splendid German-Dutch, Dutch-German expressions, until the born debater became so completely tongue-tied; that she rose from her chair and wanted to leave the room."* (September 28, 1942)

7   Looking outside from the Secret Annex is dangerous. During the day getting a breath of fresh air is also a problem. All these restrictions are not conducive to being in a good mood. *"Mrs. v.P. was in a bad mood this morning. All she did was complain, first about her cold, not being able to*

get cough drops and the agony of having to blow your nose all the time. Next she grumbled that the sun wasn't shining, the invasion hadn't started, we weren't allowed to look out the windows, etc., etc. We couldn't help but laugh at her, and it couldn't have been that bad, since she soon joined in."
(April 27, 1944)

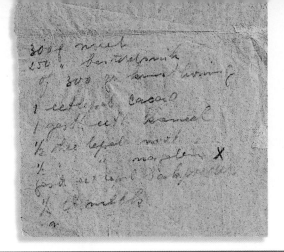

8

In November of 1942, the people in hiding and the helpers buy six large bags of dried beans. Scarcely two years later things are not going as well with the availability of food. Less and less fresh food can be found in the stores and the prices are on the rise. *"As of tomorrow, we won't have a scrap of fat, butter or margarine. Lunch today consists of mashed potatoes and pickled kale. You wouldn't believe how much kale can stink when it's a few years old!"* (March 14, 1944)

8 On various festive occasions either Auguste or Edith bakes a cake. Sometimes Miep arranges the cake, for example on Christmas and New Year's Eve 1943, with the inscription: "Peace 1944". The cake recipe was written on the back of a shopping list.

9 A menu for a dinner in the Secret Annex, on July 18, 1942, in celebration of the one year wedding anniversary of Jan and Miep Gies. With rather limited means the people in hiding are able to prepare a chic-looking meal.

Over the course of time, the table conversations become rather predictable: *"Whenever one of the eight of us opens his mouth, the other seven can finish the story for him. We know the punch line of every joke before it gets told, so that whoever's telling it is left to laugh alone. The various milkmen, grocers and butchers of the two ex-housewives have already grown beards in our eyes, so often have they been praised to the skies or pulled to pieces. There's absolutely no chance of anything new or fresh being brought up for discussion in the Annex."* (January 28, 1944)

9

Zaterdag 18 Juli 1942

D I N E R

aangeboden door "HET ACHTERHUIS"ter gelegenheid
van het eenjarig bestaan van het huwelijk van
den Weled.heer en Mevrouw G i e s.

B o u i l l o n
a la Hunzestraat
.-.-.-.-.-.-.-.-

Roastbeaf SCHOLTE
Salade Richelieu
Salade Hollandaise
1 Pomme de terre
.-.-.-.-.-.-.-.-

SAUCE DE BOEUF (JUS)
zeer miniem gebruiken svp.in verband
met verlaging v.h.boterrantsoen.
.-.-.-.-.-.-.-.-.-

RIZ a la Trautmansdorf
(Surrogaat)
.-.-.-.-.-.-.-.-.-

Suiker,Kaneel,Frambozensap
.-.-.-.-.-.-.-.-.-

KO F F I E met suiker,room
en div.verrassingen.
.-.-.-.-.-.-.-.-

There are elaborate discussions held about whether the windows may be opened a small crack at night. At first the windows are opened, but later it's considered to be too dangerous. At night all noises travel much further.

"Upstairs it sounds like thunder, but it's only Mrs. v.P.'s bed being shoved against the window so that Her Majesty, arrayed in her pink bed jacket, can sniff the night air through her delicate little nostrils." (August 4, 1943)

"One night Mrs. v.P. thought she heard loud footsteps in the attic, and she was so afraid of burglars, she woke her husband. At that very same moment, the thieves disappeared, and the only sound Mr. v.P. could hear was the frightened pounding of his fatalistic wife's heart." (March 10, 1943)

"'Oh, Putti!' (Mr. van Pels' pet name) 'They must have taken all our sausages and dried beans. And what about Peter? Oh, do you think Peter's still safe and sound in his bed?' 'I'm sure they haven't stolen Peter. Stop being such a ninny, and let me get back to sleep!' Impossible. Mrs. v.P. was too scared to sleep. A few nights later the entire Van Pels family was awakened by ghostly noises. Peter went to the attic with a flashlight and – scurry, scurry – what do you think he saw running away? A whole slew of enormous rats!" (March 10, 1943)

"His little room is – what is it really? I think it's a passageway to the attic, very narrow, very dark and damp, but... he has turned it into a real room."

February 22, 1944

Peter van Pels' Room and the Attic

Anne carefully describes Peter van Pels' small room in in her storybook.
In order to practice her writing, she creates an imaginary interview with
Peter. "My First Interview" begins with a detailed description of his room.
At first Anne doesn't think much of Peter, a boring boy. Later on she
considerably adjusts her opinion: she falls in love with him. She receives
her first kiss from him. This infatuation wears off after a little while and
Anne looks for ways to distance herself from Peter. At the moment of the
arrest, Otto Frank is giving English lessons to Peter in this room.

1

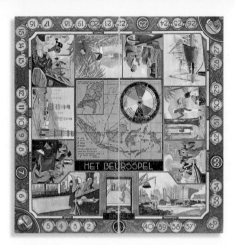

2

1. In the middle of Peter's room is the stairway that goes to the attic of the Secret Annex. This attic is the only place where he and Anne can be alone. In the attic there's a narrow stairway leading to the garret. During the hiding period, food provisions and books are kept in the attic.

   "Peter van Pels arrived at nine-thirty in the morning (while we were still at breakfast). Peter's going on sixteen, a shy, awkward boy whose company won't amount to much. Mr. and Mrs. van Pels came half an hour later." (August 14, 1942)

2. On November 8, 1942, Peter turns sixteen-years-old. Anne goes upstairs to take a look at the presents. He receives, among other things, a board game, a razor and a cigarette lighter. *"Not that he smokes so much, not at all, it just looks so distinguished."* (November 9, 1942) During the Easter holidays of 1944 the people in hiding play the stock-market board game for two afternoons straight.

→ Only in the attic can Anne and Peter spend time together alone.
During the working week, Anne comes upstairs to the attic at lunchtime
for three-quarters of an hour to get a breath of fresh air.

1 *"But...there's someone else who governs all my moods and that's...Peter.
Oh, he gazes at me with such warmth in his eyes; I don't think it will take
much for me to fall in love with him. In any case, we're getting to know each
other a little better. I wish we dared to say more. But who knows, maybe
that time will come sooner than I think! Once or twice a day he gives me
a knowing glance, I wink back and we're both happy."* (March 3, 1944)

1

2 Anne desperately longs for a kiss from Peter, a kiss that just doesn't come. She wonders if he regards her only as a pal. And if maybe he isn't in love with her after all. *"I've never been used to sharing my worries with anyone, I've never clung to a mother. But I'd love to lay my head on his shoulder and just sit there quietly."* (April 1, 1944)

3 One night she is sitting together with Peter on the couch in his room. They are leaning against each another. *"He caressed my cheek and arm, a bit clumsily, and played with my hair. Most of the time our heads were touching. How I suddenly made the right movement, I don't know, but before we went downstairs, he gave me a kiss, through my hair,*

2

3

half on my left cheek and half on my ear. I tore downstairs without looking back, and I long so much for today." (April 16, 1944)

As time goes by Anne begins to distance herself from Peter. She sees that Peter is more in need of tenderness than she is. *"He still blushes every evening when he gets his goodnight kiss, and then begs for another one. Am I merely a better substitute for Krauty? I don't mind. He's so happy, just knowing somebody loves him. After my laborious conquest, I've distanced myself a little from the situation, but you mustn't think my love has cooled. Peter's a sweetheart, but I've tightly closed the door to my inner self."* (May 19, 1944)

After the infatuation has cooled down a bit, Anne once again returns to writing about herself. Certainly in those last weeks, when she is still in a position to note things in her diary, her thoughts grow even deeper. Anne continues to turn inward and depend more and more on herself.

"I have one outstanding character trait that must be obvious to anyone who's known me for any length of time: I have a great deal of self-knowledge. In everything I do, I can watch myself as if I were a stranger. Without being biased or making excuses, I can stand across from the everyday Anne and watch what she's doing, both the good and the bad. I condemn myself in so

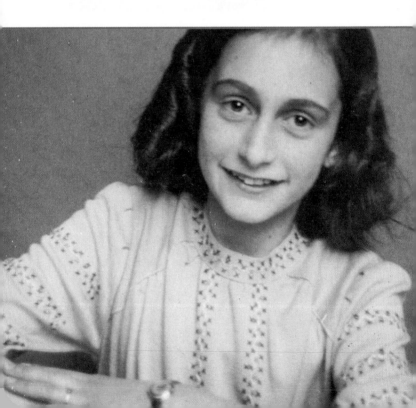

many ways that I'm beginning to realize the truth of Father's adage:
'Every child has to raise itself'." (July 15, 1944)

"I see the world gradually being turned into a wasteland, I hear the ever
approaching thunder, which will destroy us too, I feel the suffering of
millions of people and yet, if I look up into the heavens, I somehow feel that
all this will come right again, that also this savagery will stop, that there will
be peace and tranquility in the world once again. Until that time, I must
hold onto my ideals. Perhaps the day will come when I'll still be able to
realize them!" (July 15, 1944)

Two weeks later, on Tuesday August 1, 1944, Anne writes in her diary for
the last time.

The Arrest

Jo Kleiman: "On August 4, 1944, the *SD* (German Security Service of the SS) accompanied by three detectives and *SS-Oberstabsfeldwebel* Silberbauer conducted a raid. They had apparently been well-informed, forced my colleague with three guns pointed at him to show them the secret quarters where they arrested both families (8 people). Also my colleague and myself were taken away with them."

Otto Frank: "It was around ten-thirty. I was upstairs by the Van Pelses in Peter's room and I was helping him with his schoolwork, I didn't hear anything. And when I did hear something, I didn't pay any attention to it. Peter had just finished an English dictation and I had just said 'But Peter, in English double is spelled with only one b!'"

"I was showing him the mistake in the dictation when suddenly someone came running up the stairs. The stairs were squeaking, I stood up, because it was still early in the morning and everyone was supposed to be quiet – then the door opened and a man was standing right in front of us with a gun in his hand and it was pointed at us. The man was in plain clothes."

"Peter and I put up our hands. The man had us walk in front of him and ordered us to go downstairs, and he walked behind us with the pistol. Downstairs everyone was gathered. My wife, the children, the Van Pelses stood there with their hands in the air. Then Pfeffer came in, and behind him were still more strangers. In the middle of the room there was someone from the *Grüne Polizei* (Green Police). He was studying our faces."

"They then asked us where we kept our valuables? I pointed to the closet by the wall, where I had stored a small wooden chest. The man from the *Grüne Polizei* took the box, looked all around him and grabbed Anne's briefcase. He turned it upside down and shook everything inside it out; there were papers lying all over the wooden floor – notebooks and loose pages. He proceeded to put all the valuable things in the briefcase and shut it."

"Then he said: 'Get Ready. Everyone must be back here in five minutes.' The Van Pelses went upstairs to get their knapsacks, Anne and Pfeffer went to their room, and I took my knapsack which was hanging on the wall. Suddenly the man from the Grüne Polizei was standing fixated by my wife's bed staring at a locker that was between the bed and the window and he said loudly: 'Where did you get this?' He was referring to a gray footlocker with metal strips, like all of us had during World War One, and on the lid was written: Reserve Lieutenant Otto Frank. I answered: 'It belongs to me' 'What do you mean?' 'I was an officer' That really confused him. He stared at me and asked: 'Why didn't you come forward?' I bit my lip. 'They certainly would have taken that into consideration, man. You would have been sent you to Theresienstadt.'

I was silent. I just looked at him. Then he said: 'You can take your time...'"

Miep Gies: "It was August 4th. It was quiet in the office. We were working and I happened to look up. The door opened and a small man entered. He pointed the revolver in his hand at me and said: 'Stay seated! Don't move!' Of course, I was frozen with fear. He closed the door and left again. I couldn't see or hear what happened after that because I was ordered to stay at my desk. Later I heard everyone coming downstairs, very slowly. They had been able to pack in the meantime. I wasn't allowed to go to the window, I had to stay in my seat. And I did that. Afterwards Bep and I went upstairs to the bedroom of the Franks. And there we saw Anne's diary lying on the ground. 'Let's pick it up,' I said. Because Bep stood there looking around in a daze. I said: 'Pick it up, pick it up, let's get out of here,' because we were so frightened! We went downstairs and there we were, Bep and I. 'Now what Bep?' Then she said: 'You're the oldest. You should keep it.' That seemed okay."

Victor Kugler: "I heard a commotion and opened the door to my offfice to see what was going on. I saw four police officers, one was wearing a Gestapo uniform. 'Who's in charge here,' he snapped at me? I answered that I was. 'Let me see the rest of the building!' I showed him all the spaces. Then we went upstairs and were standing on the landing by the bookcase. My heart was beating very fast. The three Dutch policemen were already busy trying to open the bookcase. The moment that I had feared for years had arrived. One of the police officers pointed his gun at me and ordered me go first. The others followed behind also with their pistols drawn. The first person I saw was Mrs. Frank. I whispered 'Gestapo' to her. She sat completely still and seemed to be in shock. The others were coming downstairs from the other floors. Margot was very upset, she was crying softly."

In 1948, the police conduct an initial investigation into the betrayal and arrest of those in hiding. Willem van Maaren is one of the suspects. Van Maaren categorically denies any involvement in the betrayal. An excerpt from his March 31, 1948 testimony: "I came to work for Opekta as a warehouse-man in the spring of 1943. My activities were exclusively confined to the warehouse on the ground floor of the building.

Karl Joseph Silberbauer (left)

Willem van Maaren around 1965 (right)

However, during the year 1943-1944, I did begin to suspect that there was something unusual happening on the premises, although I didn't think about Jews in hiding. These suspicions arose because the baker, the milkman, and the green grocer were delivering rather large amounts of food provisions to the building." Van Maaren also stresses that other visitors came to the premises and that the neighbors presented a threat as well. The question of who committed the betrayal has never been answered. Nothing could be proven.

Jo Kleiman, Miep Gies, and Victor Kugler identify the Dutch *SD*-detectives as Gezinus Gringhuis and Willem Grootendorst. They are sentenced to life imprisonment. The two men say they can't remember anything about the arrest, but they do mention the name of the Austrian Karl Joseph Silberbauer, who led the action. He, himself, is interrogated during a later investigation in 1964. He declared: "I received a telephone call from my superior, with the message that someone had provided a tip about people in hiding on the Prinsengracht. I went along with a few men. There was a man working in the warehouse who responded to the question of where the Jews were hidden by pointing upstairs with his finger. We went to the second floor, where one of the supervisors of the business was working. He was immediately interrogated by one of the Dutch detectives. When he could no longer deny it, he finally pointed out the hiding place of the Jews. I admit that I entered that Annex with my pistol drawn." Silberbauer still remembers the conversation he had with Otto Frank, who had been an officer during the World War One: "He also told me," so I recall, "that he and his family, which included his daughter Anne, had spent two years in the hiding place. Because I found that hard to believe, he pointed to the pencil marks, the ones that were made by the doorpost to keep track of how much Anne had grown during the time they were in hiding."

Around one o'clock in the afternoon, an enclosed truck drives up in front of the building. The eight people in hiding, Victor Kugler, and Jo Kleiman are loaded into the truck. They are brought to the *SD*-prison on Euterpestraat. Miep Gies and Bep Voskuijl are left behind on the Prinsengracht.

After the Arrest

AUSCHWITZ

The Shoah

"The English radio says they're being gassed. I feel terribly upset."
(October 9, 1942)

On August 4, 1944, a vehicle carrying ten prisoners (the eight people in hiding and two male helpers) rides to the *Sicherheitsdienst* (*SD* or Bureau of the German Security Service of the SS) on Euterpestraat in Amsterdam. After a short interrogation, Jo Kleiman and Victor Kugler – the two helpers – are brought to the prison on Amstelveenseweg by the Germans. They are held there until September 7, 1944. There is no hearing. After four days in yet another Amsterdam prison, they are relocated to the Amersfoort transit camp. Kleiman's stomach ulcers begin hemorrhaging in the camp and this leads to his release on September 18th. At the end of September, Kugler is sent to do heavy labor with other prisoners in Zwolle and later in Wageningen. He escapes at the beginning of April 1945. Heavy penalties are attached to aiding and abetting Jews. Still, in everyday practice the enforcement of this is quite arbitrary. Miep Gies and Bep Voskuijl are not arrested. Apparently, the male arresting officers cannot imagine that these women were actually involved. They keep the business running.

The Helpers

1

1 The headquarters of the *Sicherheitsdienst* (German Security Service and Security Police) on Euterpestraat. This building also houses the Security Service jail. Miep Gies visits the prison a few days after the arrest to see if she can do anything for the imprisoned inhabitants of the Secret Annex and the helpers. Unfortunately, she is unsuccessful.

2 The prison on Amstelveenseweg. After the war, Victor Kugler points out the cell where he was held: B3-11. Jo Kleiman occupies the next cell. Six people on average inhabit a cell meant for one person. Victor Kugler and Jo Kleiman are imprisoned here for about five weeks. They stay in contact by ticking signals on the heating pipes and exchanging notes during fresh air breaks.

2

3 On September 11, 1944, Kleiman and Kugler arrive at the *Polizeiliches Durchgangslager Amersfoort* (Amersfoort Police Transit Camp). They are considered antisocial prisoners and as an indication of this receive a red circle on the back of their coats. The conditions in the camp are very severe. The Jewish prisoners are treated the worst. Thirty-five thousand people in total are imprisoned in this camp during the war.

4 Registration card of Jo Kleiman in Camp Amersfoort. The card, which is damaged immediately after the Liberation, states: "Arrival: September 11, 1944. Departure: September 18, 1944 to *Heimatort* (released to home address)." When Kleiman is released after six weeks of imprisonment, the people in hiding are already in Auschwitz. After his return, Kleiman resumes his work on the Prinsengracht. Miep Gies and Bep Voskuijl show him the diary papers of Anne Frank.

3

5 Victor Kugler's detailed registration in Camp Amersfoort. The stamp shows that on September 26, 1944, he is assigned to the *Arbeitseinsatz* (forced labor in Nazi-Germany). The stated reason for his arrest is *Judenbegünstigung* or 'helping Jews'.

5

The people in hiding are kept in the House of Detention on Wetering-
schans in Amsterdam from August 5-8, 1944. Early in the morning on
August 8, 1944 they are taken out of their cell and brought to the central
train station. Another group joins them, also Jews arrested because of
their Resistance activities or caught while in hiding. The prisoners travel
by passenger train, but as "penalty cases", to Westerbork. During this
trip, for the first time in a long time, they see the summery landscape.
After a few hours of traveling they arrive in Westerbork, located on the
heathland in Drenthe, a province of the Netherlands close to the German
border. In this transit camp, the stress of impending deportation
continually hangs in the air.

1   In the late 1930's, the Dutch government has the camp in Westerbork
built in order to house Jewish refugees fleeing Nazi Germany. On July 1,
1942, the Nazi occupying force turns it into a *Polizeiliches Durchgangs-*

The People in Hiding

1

lager, a police transit camp enroute to the camps in Germany and Poland. In 1942 and 1943, most of the Jews living in the Netherlands are deported via this camp "to the East". Exactly what this destination entails is not known to them. By 1944, the camp primarily houses people who have been spared deportation or those who have been arrested while in hiding, like Anne and the others.

2   The S-Barrack # 67 at Westerbork houses the "penalty-cases", who wear a red piece of fabric on their camp clothing. In retrospect, the situation of the former inhabitants of the Secret Annex does not differ much from others in the camp.

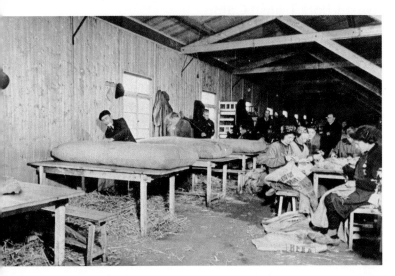

2

Life in Westerbork transit camp revolves around the deportation train. From the summer of 1942 until the spring of 1943, a train departs "to the East" almost every Tuesday, each time crammed with hundreds, even thousands of people. At a later date, the transports decrease in both frequency and size. Experiencing unbearable tension, everyone in the camps awaits the reading of the new list of deportees. In total, 100,000 Jews are deported from Westerbork. About 245 Roma and Sinti (Gypsies) are also deported from Westerbork. Initially, the precise destinations are not known. Most of the trains go to the extermination camps Sobibor and Auschwitz. Bergen-Belsen and Theresienstadt are other destinations.

1 A transport departing from Westerbork. The train journey takes a few days. In closed boxcars without windows, with far too many people in a much too small space, with hardly any water and food, without fresh air and without toilets.

Westerbork Transit Camp

1

2 Part of the list of the 83rd *Judentransport* (transport of Jews) from Westerbork to "the East", on September 3, 1944. This transport, which included the inhabitants of the Secret Annex, was the last transport from Westerbork to Auschwitz. There are 1019 people on this train; 498 men, 442 women and 79 children, all Jewish according to Nazi criteria.

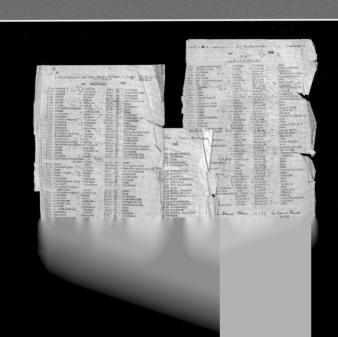

1 Arrival and "selection" of Hungarian Jews in Auschwitz-Birkenau, May 1944.

"I can no longer talk about how I felt when my family arrived on the train platform in Auschwitz and we were forcibly separated from each other." (Otto Frank, 1979)

Auschwitz-Birkenau

Of the eight people in hiding, Hermann van Pels is the first to die. He arrives with the others in Auschwitz on the night of September 5, 1944. A "selection" takes place immediately. The men are separated from the women. Children younger than fifteen, the elderly, people who are weak and sick are immediately gassed. The others, including for the time being all the inhabitants of the Secret Annex, are transferred to work camps. Here they come in contact with a system aimed at dehumanizing people: their heads are shaven bald, they receive camp clothes, and a number is tattooed on their arm. The male Secret Annex inhabitants receive a number between B-9108 and B-9365. A prisoner is referred to by his or her number. Hermann van Pels is assigned to a commando unit (forced-labor group) that works outdoors. A few weeks later he is gassed. At that time, he is 54 years old. The precise date of his death is unknown.

1 Registration card of Hermann van Pels, from the administration of the Jewish Council in Westerbork. After the Liberation, the Dutch Red Cross confiscated

Hermann van Pels

1

2

the registration-card file boxes from Westerbork to be able to provide information about deportees. Written on this card in red pencil is the date S 3-9-44, on which Herman van Pels was transported from Westerbork to Auschwitz.

Auschwitz-Birkenau is an extermination camp. The mass murder here is organized by the Nazis in an industrialized fashion. In September 1941, the Nazis begin using gas chambers. The Shoah is the genocide of the Jews, the murder of a people on an unprecedented scale. In Auschwitz-Birkenau alone, the Nazis killed more than one million Jews. Exact figures are not known because the people who were gassed immediately upon their arrival were never registered.

2 Auschwitz-Birkenau, May 1944. All the baggage and clothing belonging to those who are murdered in the gas chambers is sorted by the other prisoners.

Fritz Pfeffer is just one of the prisoners transferred from Auschwitz to another camp. Prisoners continue to hope that life will be better somewhere else. Fritz Pfeffer also harbors these same hopes. In October 1944, he signs up for a doctor's transport leaving Auschwitz. He ends up in Neuengamme, a concentration camp near Hamburg. This camp has more than eighty outdoor commando units operating; sixty for male prisoners and twenty for female prisoners. All are engaged in doing heavy forced labor. The abominable working conditions, the poor clothing, the inadequate nutrition, the lack of health care and hygiene, and abuse by the SS and camp guards result in the death of many prisoners. These deaths are part and parcel of the deliberate policy of the Nazis to kill people through the use of forced labor. Fritz Pfeffer dies in Neuengamme's sick-bay barrack on December 20, 1944 at the age of fifty-five.

Fritz Pfeffer

1

2

201

1 Fritz Pfeffer's card from the records of the Jewish Council in Westerbork.

2 Neuengamme, around 1941.

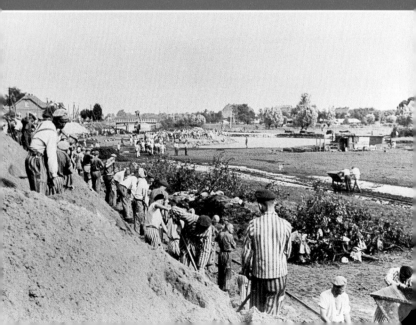

202

Edith Frank, her daughters, and the other new female arrivals spend
their first few days in Auschwitz "in quarantine". The arms of the 212
Dutch women from the September 3, 1944 transport are tattooed
with numbers ranging from A-25060 to A-25271. After the quarantine,
most of the women – so probably including Edith, Margot and Anne
– are assigned to commando units (forced-labor groups). The Frank
women end up in a barrack with many other Dutch women.
Survivors later relate that there is a very strong bond between the
mother and her daughters. Apparently, the bickering between Anne
and Edith has been relegated to the past. At the end of October,
when a large number of Dutch women are transferred to a labor
camp in Liebau (Upper Silesia) Edith remains behind with her sick
daughters. A few days later a new selection takes place. Margot and
Anne are put on a transport to Bergen-Belsen concentration camp
and Edith must say goodbye to her daughters. At the end of November,

Edith Frank-Holländer

DOSS: 117.265

FRANK-HOLLÄNDER, Edith Sara

geb.16-1-1900 Aken

Merwedeplein 37 '' Amsterdam

zonder

N.I.

zonder

gehuwd   man: Frank,Otto Heinrich Isr.
                    12.5.1889
           dochter:Frank,Margot Betti Sar
                    16-2-1926
                 '' Frank,Annelies Marie S
                    12.6.1929

6-1-45 te Bakenau

1   2

203

Edith ends up in the sick-bay barrack. She dies there on January 6, 1945 at the age of forty-four.

1 Edith Frank's card from the records of the Jewish Council in Westerbork.

2 Auschwitz-Birkenau, 1945.

At first, Margot Frank is together with her sister and mother in Auschwitz. At the end of October 1944, the Soviet forces advance on Poland, where the camp is located. The Nazis bring as many prisoners as possible back to Germany, especially those prisoners who are still able to work. Margot and Anne Frank are selected for transport to Bergen-Belsen. They supposedly leave Auschwitz by train on October 28, 1944, in boxcars squeezed full with 1,306 other women, enroute to Bergen-Belsen. This could have also occurred on November 1, 1944, in an evacuation transport with 634 other women. A train journey of four days; once again in freight cars crammed full of people, with little food or water. From the train station in Celle, the prisoners have to walk many miles to the Bergen-Belsen camp. When the prisoners from Auschwitz arrive, Bergen-Belsen is already more than full. The conditions there are awful, there is a shortage of everything, and contagious diseases are running rampant.

Margot Frank

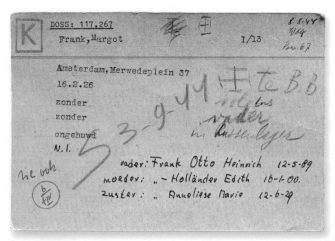

1

2

A few months later, in March 1945, Margot Frank dies of typhus and deprivation in Bergen-Belsen. She has just turned nineteen years old. The exact date of her death is unknown.

1 Margot Frank's card from the records of the Jewish Council in Westerbork.

2 Women's barrack in Bergen-Belsen shortly after the liberation of the camp. About 8,000 women from Auschwitz-Birkenau arrive in Bergen-Belsen during October and November 1944. At the time of its liberation, the camp still houses about 56,000 people who are starving and ill. Ten-thousand bodies have not yet been buried. A total of 80,000 people die in this camp.

During the selection on the train platform in Auschwitz, Anne Frank escapes the gas chambers. Along with Margot, Edith and other new arrivals she is first placed "in quarantine". Following this, the prisoners are usually appointed to a commando unit. An opportunity to rest after working does not really exist. The barracks are filled with wooden plank beds crammed full with people. The endless roll-calls are deathly tiring. After a few weeks Anne falls ill. Together with Margot, they are admitted to a separate barrack housing sick prisoners. Here the risk of being selected for the gas chambers is very high. At the end of October or beginning of November 1944, the Frank sisters are evacuated to the German concentration camp Bergen-Belsen. Their mother, Edith, remains behind. From the well-organized death factory of Auschwitz they arrive at a huge, poorly organized, chaotic camp. Thirst and hungar are pervasive in Bergen-Belsen. There is no adequate sanitation. Epidemics claim thousands of victims. Anne survives for a little over four months in Bergen-Belsen, finally succumbing to typhus and deprivation.

Anne Frank

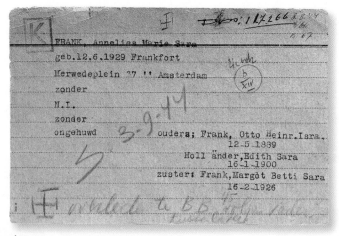

1

2

She dies in March 1945 at the age of fifteen, just a few weeks before the liberation of the camp and a few days after Margot dies. The exact date of Anne's death is not known.

1 Anne Frank's card from the records of the Jewish Council in Westerbork.

2 Hannah Goslar, a friend of Anne's from the years before going into hiding, in a photograph taken in 1996. Beginning in February 1944, Hannah is placed in the *Sternlager* and that is where she hears, at a certain moment, that Anne Frank is with the women in the tent camp. *"So I went to the barbed wire, but that was forbidden and the Germans kept watch from the tower. I waited until it got dark and went there and started to call out. I received an answer from Mrs. van Pels. She said immediately to me: 'You want Anne.' She went to get Anne; Margot was already very sick."*

3 Bergen-Belsen shortly after its liberation. Hannah Goslar: *"Anne thought that her parents were dead. I have always thought if Anne had known that her father was still alive, she would have found the strength to go on living."*

On the train platform in Auschwitz, Gusti van Pels is separated from her husband and son. She probably also loses contact with Edith, Anne and Margot rather quickly. The many thousands of prisoners are split-up into different camps all cordoned off by barbed wire. Gusti van Pels' residence barrack and commando unit in Auschwitz are not known. She is transferred on November 26, 1944 to Bergen-Belsen. Here she sees Margot and Anne Frank once again. Gusti is the one who arranges the meeting between Anne and Hannah Goslar. On February 6, 1945, Gusti is transported again, to the Raguhn commando, an outdoor commando unit of Buchenwald concentration camp. She probably works there until Raguhn is evacuated and the prisoners are taken to Theresienstadt. Auguste van Pels dies in April or May 1945, on her way to or shortly after arriving in Theresienstadt. At the time of her death, she is forty-four years old.

Auguste van Pels

1

2

1 Auguste van Pels's card from the records of the Jewish Council in Westerbork.

2 Transport of prisoners to Theresienstadt, 1942.

Peter van Pels probably spends a few weeks in Auschwitz together with his father. In October or November 1944 he sees his father being taken off to the gas chamber. Peter works in the postal department, which is less severe than working in one of the outdoor commando units. Because of this job, he sometimes comes across extra food which he shares with Otto Frank and other prisoners. Sometime around January 20, 1945, the advancing Russian army is so close to Auschwitz that the SS decides to flee the camp. They have already dismantled the gas chambers in November. They now try to destroy the camp archives and they take prisoners along with them when they leave. During these evacuations, quite often by foot, many prisoners die. The details of Peter van Pels' evacuation journey are not known. He is probably still transported by train or truck, because he arrives in Mauthausen on January 25, 1945. He dies there on May 5, 1945, the day of the Liberation. He is eighteen years old.

Peter van Pels

1   2

1 Peter van Pels' card from the records of the Jewish Council in Westerbork.

2 Prisoners in one of Mauthausen's barracks, May 6, 1945.

Otto Frank is the only one of the eight people in hiding who survives the camps. Even he cannot explain it. *"I was blessed with luck, and many friends,"* he writes to his mother about this. After enduring several months of heavy labor in one of Auschwitz's outdoor commando units, Otto is finally completely exhausted. Thanks to the intervention of a doctor he ends up in the sick-bay barrack. There certainly isn't any medical care but at least he doesn't have to work anymore. Peter van Pels visits Otto Frank daily and cares for him. He also visits Otto shortly before the evacuation of Auschwitz, sometime around January 20, 1945, and insists that Otto should also come along. But he doesn't have any strength left to make the trip. It is exactly this that leads to his salvation. The Soviet army liberates Auschwitz on January 27, 1945. Otto is one of the 7,560 prisoners that has remained behind. After a journey home lasting several months, he finally arrives back in the Netherlands in June 1945.

Otto Frank

1

2

215

1 Otto Frank's card from the records of the Jewish Council in Westerbork. "Returned!" is later written on the card by a Red Cross worker. The exclamation mark indicates just how exceptional this was. Only 5,200 people return from the camps in the East.

2 Liberated prisoners standing in front of the sick-bay barrack in Auschwitz.

1 In this cloth satchel, Otto Frank keeps the few things that he leaves Auschwitz with: a needle with a few threads, some pieces of paper.

2 During the journey home, lasting so many months because everything is in chaos after the war, Otto makes notations in this small notebook.

3 Otto Frank's repatriation card, an important document needed for traveling. He arrives back in Amsterdam on June 3, 1945, more than four months after his liberation from Auschwitz.

On July 7, 1945, Otto Frank writes to his second cousin Milly Stanfield: *"I have to take the fact of Edith's fate but I still hope to find my children and that is at the moment all I live for...I waver between hope and fear..."* On July 21st, he writes to his mother and brothers that he has heard that Margot and Anne died in Bergen-Belsen.

"Daily I tried to speak to people about the girls. I spoke to quite a number who met them in Bergen-Belsen in Jan./Febr. but I could not trace them any further. Now I know all the truth." (Otto Frank)

"The friends here could save some photos and the diary of Anne. I had it in my hands but I couldn't read it yet." (Otto Frank)

RÉPUBLIQUE FRANÇAISE

CARTE DE RAPATRIÉ

Nom: FRANK — Prénoms: Otto — Sexe: M

Etat Civil: M. 2. — Profession: Commerçant en gros

Date de naissance: 12.6.89 — Lieu de naissance: Francfort s/Mein

Nom du Père: Michael — Nom de la Mère: Sterne Alice

Nationalité d'origine: Allemand — Nationalité actuelle: Hollandais

Dernière affectation militaire en France: Hollandais

HOLLANDE

PHOTO 4 × 4

VÊTEMENTS

TICKETS — TABAC

1061874

3

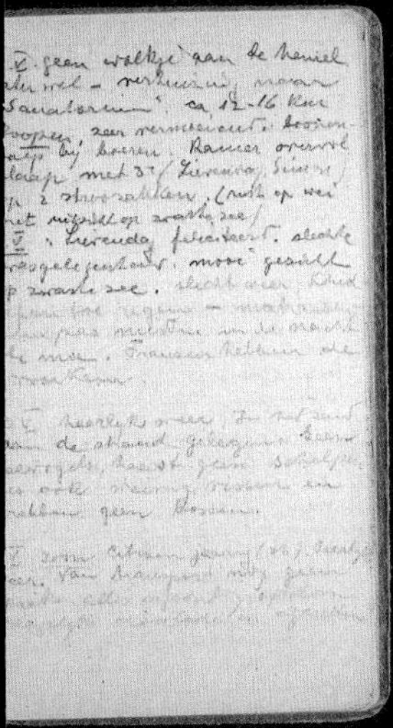

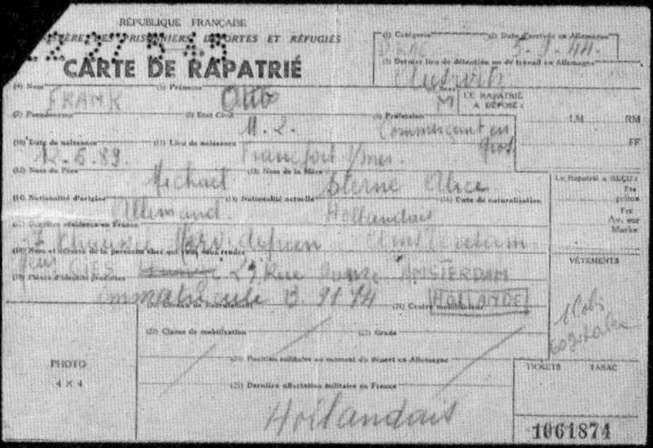

Anne Frank's Diaries

"You've known for a long time that my greatest wish is to be a journalist and later on, a famous writer. In any case, after the war I'd like to publish a book called 'The Secret Annex'." (May 11, 1944)

1 Anne Frank receives this diary on June 12, 1942, just before going into hiding. She immediately begins to use it. In the beginning, she mainly writes about her experiences at school. She also describes every pupil in her class in a few lines. It is a diary like many girls keep and have kept. Much attention is paid to boys, school and girlfriends. On the first page, she writes: *"I hope I will be able to confide everything to you, as I have never been able to confide in anyone, and I hope you will be a great source of comfort and support."* (June 12, 1942)

2 A few weeks later the Frank family has to to go into hiding, in effect, to escape persecution. Anne reads a lot during the hiding period. Every other week, Jo Kleiman brings along some girl's books for her to read. *"I'm enthusiastic about the Joop ter Heul series. I've enjoyed all of Cissy van Marxveldt's books very much. I've read The Zaniest Summer four times, and the ludicrous situations still make me laugh."* (September 21, 1942)

3 Anne also writes a large number of short stories in the period from July 1943 to May 1944. In the beginning these stories are primarily centered around things that happen during the hiding period. Later, she also writes a number of fairy tales and story lines for novels. *"A few weeks ago I started writing a story, something I made up from beginning to end, and I've enjoyed it so much that the products of my pen are piling up."* (August 7, 1943)

4 Anne is even already planning to send one of her fairy tales to a magazine for publication. *"I want to ask the magazine 'The Prince' if they'll take one of my fairytales, under a pseudonym, of course. But up to now all my fairytales have been too long, so I don't think I have much of a chance."* (April 21, 1944)

3

De Prins

1 On March 28, 1944, the people in hiding listen to the radio broadcast of the Dutch government in exile in England. Minister Bolkestein urges listeners to save personal documents about the war. The people in hiding immediately point to Anne's diary. Anne, herself, also immediately starts to fantasize about a novel entitled "The Secret Annex". She thinks the title sounds intriguing, as if it were a detective novel.

Sometime around May 20, 1944, Anne begins the actual work on The Secret Annex. In approximately ten weeks, she rewrites a large part of the original version of her diary onto loose sheets of paper. She now consistently directs all correspondence to just one imaginary friend: Kitty. *"At long last after a great deal of reflection I have started my 'Achterhuis', in my head it is as good as finished, although it won't go as quickly as that really, if it ever comes off at all."* (May 20, 1944)

225

2 During the short period between May 20, 1944 and her arrest on August 4, 1944, Anne revises and edits her original diary. Sometimes there are small corrections in the text and sometimes she omits complete passages, for example, regarding her sexuality. In addition to this, Anne also continues to keep her daily diary.

3 The last loose sheet containing rewritten text is dated March 29, 1944. Up until that day, Anne makes headway in revising the original version of her diary. In ten weeks time, Anne fills an average of four or five pages per day.

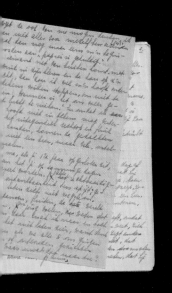

3

The Publication of the Diary

"I want to be useful or bring enjoyment to all people. I want to go on living even after my death! And therefore I am so grateful to God for giving me this gift of writing, of expressing all that is in me!" (March 25, 1944)

In the middle of July 1945, when Otto hears the terrible news that both his daughters have died in the camps, Miep Gies hands him Anne's notebooks with the words: *"Here is your daughter Anne's legacy to you."* Otto informs his family in the United States and England, as well as his mother and sister in Switzerland, about the death of Anne and Margot. In a letter he writes to his mother on August 22, 1945, he mentions Anne's diary for the first time: *"As luck would have it, Miep was able to rescue an photo album and Anne's diary. I didn't have the strength to read it."* But once he begins reading the diary, he cannot put it down.

1 Otto Frank in his office on Prinsengracht 1954. The tattooed number on his arm is clearly visible.

Otto makes a transcript of Anne's texts with his revisions. He uses, as he later explains, "what's most important" from the diary. He leaves

out, as far as he's concerned, the uninteresting parts and personal observations that "are nobody elses's business". Otto shortens Anne's text and translates it into German. This version is sent to his mother in Basel who doesn't understand Dutch.

2 Following the completion of the shortened version for his mother, Otto makes a new and more extensive transcript on his typewriter. Otto has a few close friends read the corrected text.

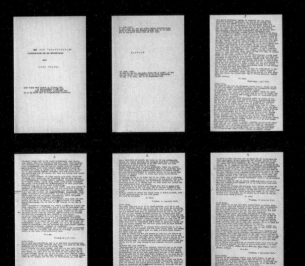

230

1 The manuscript is given to the historian and Dutch scholar, Dr. Annie Romein-Verschoor, who passes it on to her husband, the historian Dr. Jan Romein. Both of them are deeply impressed by the diary. Dr. Romein writes a front page article entitled *Kinderstem* or 'A Child's Voice', for the widely circulated daily Dutch newspaper *Het Parool*, formerly a Resistance newpaper. In it he concludes: *"It is clear to me that in this seemingly inconsequential child's diary, all the hideousness of fascism is embodied, more so than in all the evidence presented at Nuremberg put together."* This article attracts much attention. Also from the publishing company, Contact.

2 Noted in Otto Frank's datebook on June 25, 1947 is the word: "BOOK".

3 Anne Frank's book, *The Secret Annex: Diary Letters from June 14, 1942 to August 1, 1944*, is published on June 25, 1947 in an edition of 1,500 copies.

With this, Otto Frank succeeds in fulfilling the wish of his daughter. The book is very well received in the Netherlands. The first Dutch edition is quickly sold out. In December 1947, a second edition is issued. In the United States the manuscript is initially rejected by a dozen or so publishers. Finally in 1952, *The Diary of a Young Girl* is published in both the United States and England.

232

4   In the years that follow, translations are published in countries such as:
    Japan, East Germany, Switzerland, Italy, Denmark, Sweden, Norway,
    Finland, Iceland, Spain, Argentina, Mexico, Uruguay, Portugal, Brazil,
    Greece, Turkey, Hungary, Poland, Rumania, the Soviet Union,
    Czechoslovakia, Yugoslavia, Israel, India, South Korea and Thailand.

5   Otto Frank receives tens-of-thousands of letters from youngsters.
    All during those years, up until his death on August 19, 1980, he devotes
    a few hours a day to answering these letters together with his second
    wife Fritzi Frank-Markovits. In 1979, the year before he dies, he writes:
    *"I have received many thousands of letters. Young people especially
    always want to know how these terrible things could ever have happened.
    I answer them as well as I can. And then at the end, I often finish by saying:
    'I hope that Anne's book will have an effect on the rest of your life so that*

insofar as it is possible in your own circumstances, you will work for unity and peace.'"

1 In the United States, preparations for a stage play based on Anne's diary begin in 1953. In the photograph (from left to right): Jo Kleiman, Mrs. Frank-Markovits, the couple Hackett-Goodrich (the creators of the stage adaption), Otto Frank next to Garson Kanin, the play's director. The stage adaption strays from the book in many aspects. Still, Otto feels that the essence of the diary has been left sufficiently intact and he agrees to the production.

The premiere of the play takes place on October 5, 1955, at the Cort Theatre in New York City. Otto Frank is not present and in a letter he apologizes to the actors: *"You will all realize that for me this play is a part of my life, and the idea that my wife and children as well as I will be presented on the stage is a painful one to me. Therefore it is impossible for me to come and see it. I assure you that my thoughts are with everyone of you."* The play is critically acclaimed in the

reviews and becomes a huge success on Broadway running
for 717 performances.

Many theatre companies throughout Europe and elsewhere in the world
include the play in their repertoire. In 1995, the play is partially revised
by Wendy Kesselman. The historical context and the character develop-
ment of Anne receive more attention, along with the fact that it revolves
around Jews.

2 Shooting of the feature film "The Diary of Anne Frank" begins in 1958.
   The director is George Stevens. The American cover girl Millie Perkins
   portrays Anne Frank. The Secret Annex is copied in detail and recon-
   structed on a set in Beverly Hills. The film is well received, earning it
   three Oscars that year. Yet, it is not a box-office success. However, all this
   attention results once again in renewed worldwide interest for the book.

2   1

The diary achieves international critical acclaim. Anne's diary is a moving testimony against the evil of National Socialism. For millions of people this book is their first encounter with the Holocaust. This leads neo-Nazis to claim that the book is a fake. As early as 1957, publications containing these sorts of allegations start appearing. Neo-Nazis also deny that the Holocaust ever occurred. They hope, in this way, to rid National Socialism of its criminal character and present it as a respectable political movement. Otto Frank also devotes part of his time to court cases against neo-Nazis who claim that the diary is a forgery. He wins each and every court case. After his death in 1980, Otto Frank leaves the notebooks of his daughter to the Dutch State, which arranges a scientific examination of the writings. An important aspect of the study is the graphological analysis of Anne's handwriting, which proves without a doubt that the diary is authentic.

3 Sculpture of Anne Frank in Utrecht, 1987.

The diary of Anne Frank has been read by millions of people throughout the world, making it the most translated Dutch book of all time. Anne Frank appeals to people from all sorts of cultures and lifestyles. Obviously there are elements in the diary that are universally recognizable by young and old.

"One single Anne Frank moves us more than the countless others who suffered just as she did but whose faces have remained in the shadows. Perhaps it is better that way; if we were capable of taking in all the suffering of all those people, we would not be able to live." (Primo Levi, writer and survivor of Auschwitz)

"Some of us read Anne Frank's diary on Robben Island and derived much encouragement from it." (Nelson Mandela, president of South Africa, 1994)

"Of the multitude who throughout history have spoken for human dignity in times of great suffering and loss, no voice is more compelling than that of Anne Frank." (John F. Kennedy, president of the United States, 1961)

The Anne Frank House

In 1957, 263 Prinsengracht, the location of the hiding place, is threatened with demolition. This plan is thwarted thanks to the initiative of a few of Amsterdam's residents. The Anne Frank House organization is founded and they purchase the building. Otto Frank is appointed to the Board of Trustees. After the restoration of the building, the Secret Annex opens as a museum on May 3, 1960. This photograph of Otto Frank is taken in the attic of the museum a few hours before the opening. Yet, Otto Frank wants to do more than just open the Secret Annex to the public. He establishes his own educational foundation, enabling youngsters from all over the world to come in contact with each other. Otto Frank is a regular visitor to these conferences in the Anne Frank House, which address a diversity of topics like: the relationship between Judaism and Christianity, discrimination, prejudice and war. For visitors, scale models depicting the situation in the house during the hiding period are placed on exhibit in the Secret Annex. Visits become so numerous (about 180,000 visitors in 1970) that a structural rebuilding of the house is necessary. In the 1970's exhibitions are mounted about Jewish persecution between 1933 and 1945 and on contemporary human rights violations. The first traveling exhibition about anti-Semitism in the early 1980's is followed in 1985 with "Anne Frank in the World, 1929-1945". All over the world, this traveling exhibition attracts many visitors. Educational work related to Anne Frank, anti-Semitism, racism and prejudice is extended – nationally and internationally.

By the early 1990s, it appears that expansion of the museum is necessary to better receive and inform the increasing number of visitors about the conditions in which Anne Frank's diary was written. In November 1993, the City of Amsterdam gives the go ahead for the project "Preservation and the Future of the Anne Frank House". During extensive rebuilding activities that last until the summer of 1999, the Secret Annex remains open to visitors. A new building, designed by the architectural firm Benthem Crouwel, is constructed on the site of the former student housing. The neighboring building at # 265 Prinsengracht is renovated. As a result of the reconstruction, the front part of the house at # 263 Prinsengracht, where the hiding place was located, is largely returned to the atmosphere and style of the hiding period. Here is where the helpers worked and where the people in hiding also came outside of working hours. For this reconstruction, photographs taken by Maria Austria (in 1957) provided much to go by, just like the floorplans from 1957.

"The preservation of the Secret Annex is a sum total of details," states Professor Temminck Groll, "doorhandles, light switches, curtains, lamps, wallpaper, and floor covering. The entire atmosphere of the building at 263 Prinsengracht has become more somber. The old colors in the Secret Annex served as the sampler for the front part of the house. So here there is also more of a feeling of the 1940's; as it is now, we almost expect to see the people in hiding wandering through the house on Sundays and outside of weekly working hours!"

"Restoration and the design and layout of a museum go hand in hand. It is important to clearly show what is authentic and what has been added. For this reason we have clearly indicated all the breakthroughs between the buildings that were not originally present. Both in the front part of the house and the Secret Annex, the space plays an essential role in enabling viewers to be transported back in time to the hiding period. The quotations from Anne Frank's diary provide further information about the rooms and the objects."
(Marijke van der Wijst, Museum Designer)

"In the new building of the Anne Frank House one is struck by the transparent and open atmosphere, and that is also the intention. The typical Amsterdam design that divides a house into a front part and a back annex with a courtyard in the middle to catch the daylight has been echoed in this new building. The visitor, who has just come face to face with the past, can catch his or her breath here. The spacious exhibition room is suitable for the contemporary themes that the Anne Frank House wants to address."
(Mels Crouwel, architect new building)

"I see the world gradually being turned into a wasteland, I hear the ever approaching thunder, which will destroy us too, I feel the suffering of millions of people and yet, if I look up into the heavens, I somehow feel that this will come right again, that also this savagery will stop, that there will be peace and tranquility in the world once again. Until that time, I must hold onto my ideals. Perhaps the day will come when I'll still be able to realize them."
(Anne Frank, July 15, 1944)

Appendix

Pen Names

When Anne Frank rewrites her diary with the idea of publishing it, she creates a pseudonym for all the central characters. Otto Frank chooses to retain part of these pen names in the 1947 publication of the diary. In the Critical Edition of 1985 all the actual names are published. In the new version of the diary published in 1991 some of the people in hiding still have pen names, but the helpers once again have their real names. In this catalogue everyone is referred to by their actual name.

Actual Name	Pen Name
Anne Frank	Anne Frank
Margot Frank	Margot Frank
Otto Frank ('Pim')	Otto Frank
Edith Frank	Edith Frank
Hermann van Pels	Mr. Van Daan
Auguste van Pels	Mrs. Van Daan
Peter van Pels	Peter van Daan
Fritz Pfeffer	Mr. Dussel
Jo Kleiman	Mr. Koophuis
Victor Kugler	Mr. Kraler
Bep Voskuijl	Elli Vossen
Johan Voskuijl	Mr. Vossen
Miep Gies	Miep van Santen
Jan Gies	Henk van Santen

Photography Credits

Abbreviations

AB	Allard Bovenberg, Amsterdam
AFF	Anne Frank Fonds, Basel
AFS	Anne Frank Stichting, Amsterdam
AN	Arnold Newman
Coll.vB	Van Beusekom Collection
Coll.G	Gies Collection
Coll.V	Visser Collection
Coll.vW	Van Wijk Collection
GB	Gon Buurman
GBW	Galerie Bilderwelt, Reinhard Schultz, Berlin
HNP	Harry Naef Pressebilder, Zürich
IWM	Imperial War Museum, London
JH	Juul Hondius
KB	Karel Bönnekamp
KLM	KLM Aerocarto
LH	Linda Hirsch
MA	Maria Austria Instituut, Amsterdam
MV	Maarten van de Velde
NA	National Archives, Washington DC
NFA	Nederlands Fotoarchief, Rotterdam
	(Violette Cornelius)
NRK	Informatiebureau Nederlandse Rode Kruis, coll. Oorlogsarchief
NIOD	Nederlands Instituut voor Oorlogsdocumentatie, Amsterdam
PC	Private Collection
PL	P. Lust
PMO	Panstwowe Muzeum Oswiecim
SF	Spaarnestad Fotoarchief
TMM	Terezin Memorial Museum
USHMM	United States Holocaust Memorial Museum, Washington DC
VM	Verzetsmuseum Amsterdam
W	Erven H.J. Wijnne
YV	Yad Vashem, Jeruzalem

Some of the photographs used in this publication have origins that cannot be traced with certainty. Those who discover their own photos here may contact the Anne Frank House.

251

Colophon

Publication and Production Anne Frank House,
Anneke Boekhoudt, Nico de Bruijn,
Mieke Sobering

Compilation and Editing Anne Frank House,
Menno Metselaar, Ruud van der Rol, Dineke Stam

Final Editing Hansje Galesloot

Photo Archive Anne Frank House, Yt Stoker

Illustration Eric van Rootselaar

Corrections Miriam Gerretzen

Translation Epicycles, Amsterdam,
Lorraine T. Miller

Design Beukers Scholma, Haarlem

Lithography Grafisch Produktie Bureau,
Lia Durrer

Printing PlantijnCasparie Schiedam/Rotterdam,
Paul Melchers, Colette Spek-Lansbergen

With Thanks to J.J. van Borssum Waalkes,
Buddy Elias, Henry Giersthove, Miep Gies,
Paul Gies, Arnold Newman, W.F. van Tellingen,
M. Wijnne-Rouma

ISBN 90 72972 53 8

Refurnishing Museum Anne Frank House,
Wouter van der Sluis, Gerrit Netten

Acquisitions Refurnishing David Peters,
NOB Props, Rein van der Pol

Photographs Refurnishing Allard Bovenberg

Anne Frank House
Prinsengracht 263, Amsterdam
P.O. Box 730, 1000 AS Amsterdam
The Netherlands
www.annefrank.nl